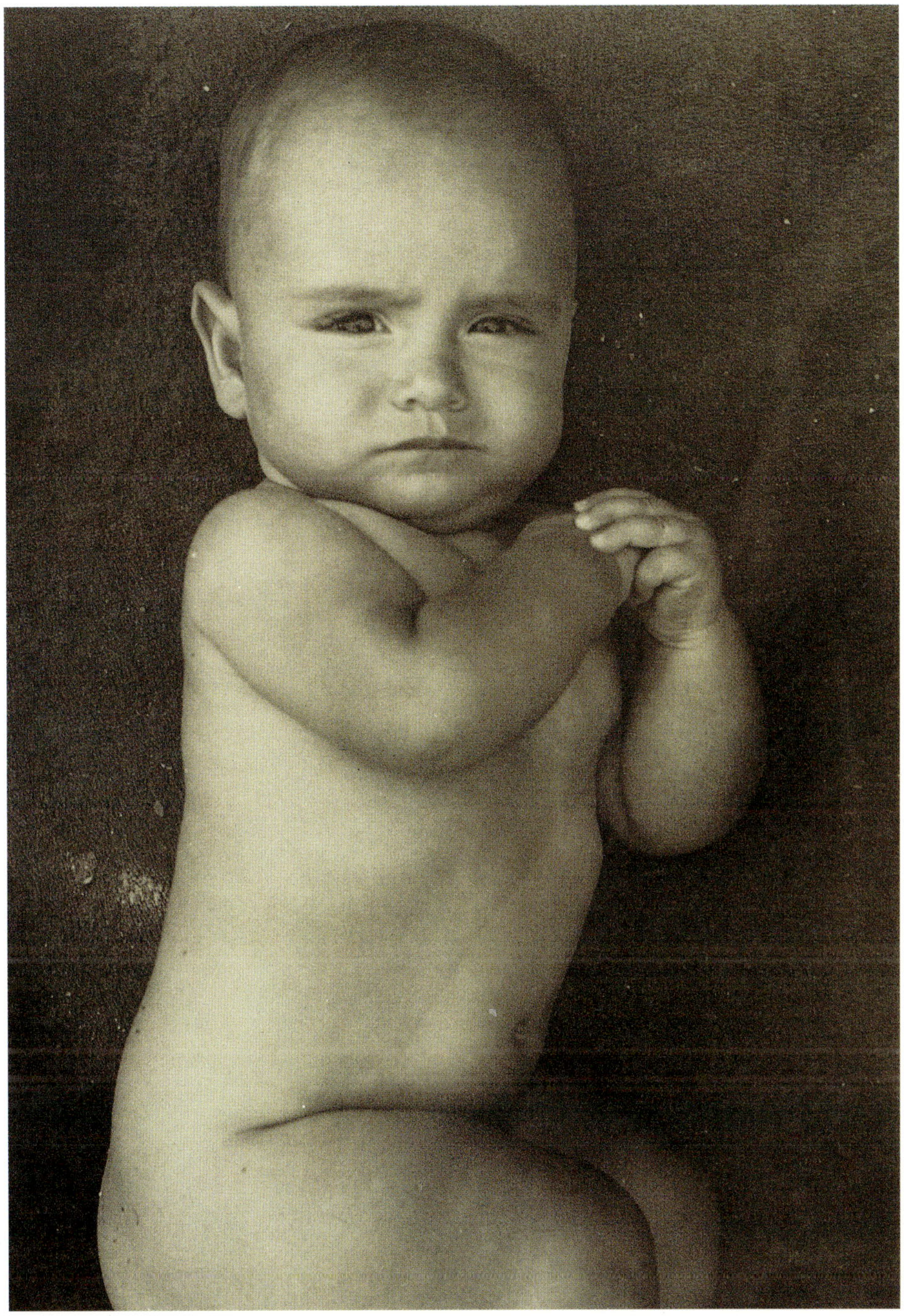

STELLA 1978

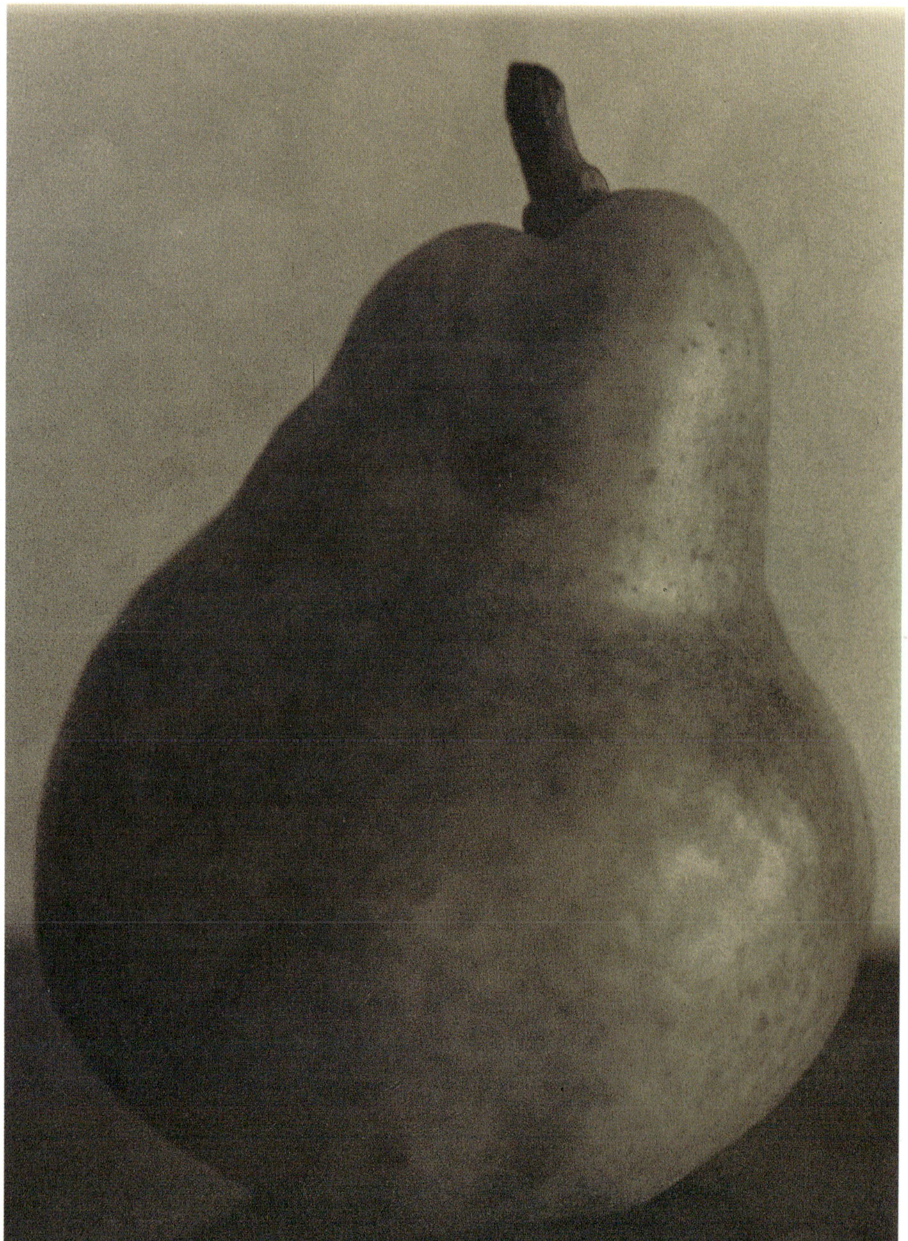

GOLDEN PEAR 1977

SHEILA METZNER

COLOR

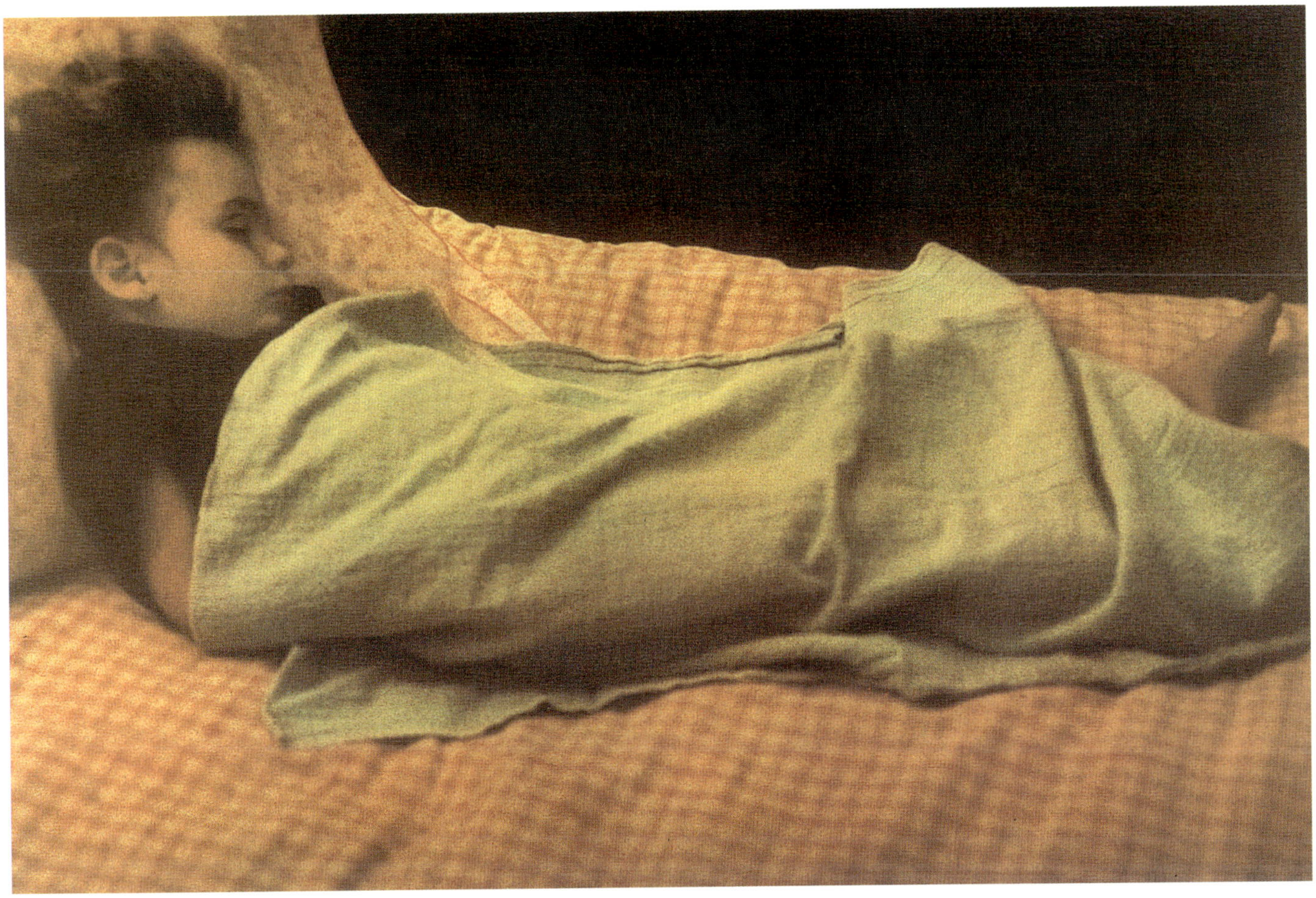

STELLA ON FIRE 1982

THERE WAS NO MORE BEAUTIFUL THING IN THE WORLD THAN THE PALACE OF THE EMPEROR OF CHINA. IT WAS BUILT OF THE VERY FINEST PORCELAIN, DELICATE AND FRAGILE AS AN EGG-SHELL. THE PEOPLE, HIGH AND LOW, WHO DWELT IN THAT PALACE MOVED WITH THE UTMOST GRACE AND CARE LEST THEY SHOULD BREAK ANYTHING, AND IN THIS THEY HAD MORE ADMIRATION FOR THE EXTREME BEAUTY OF THE PLACE THAN FEAR OF BEING TRAMPLED UPON BY THE EMPEROR FOR ANY DAMAGE CAUSED BY CLUMSINESS. THE PALACE GARDEN WAS SO BIG THAT NOT EVEN THE HEAD GARDENER COULD TELL YOU WHERE IT ENDED.

IT CONTAINED THE MOST WONDERFUL FLOWERS; EVERY HERE AND THERE AMONG THE GLORIOUS BLOOMS WAS ONE MORE RARE THAN ITS NEIGHBORS; AND, AS IF TO ATTRACT YOUR ATTENTION TO ITS SPLENDOR, EACH HAD ATTACHED TO IT A LITTLE SILVER BELL WHICH TINKLED MELODIOUSLY IN THE HANDS OF EVERY PASSING ZEPHYR. MILES AND MILES AND MILES OF BEAUTIFUL TREES AND FLOWERS, WITH SMOOTH LAWNS AND SPARKLING FOUNTAINS; AND ALWAYS, IF YOU WISHED, YOU COULD TURN OFF INTO A DELIGHTFUL WOOD WHICH SKIRTED THE GARDEN AND LED DOWN A GENTLE SLOPE TO THE SEA, WHERE, ON THE BRINK, THE TREES WERE SO HIGH AND SPREADING, AND THE BLUE WATER BENEATH SO SUDDENLY DEEP AND

STILL, THAT GREAT SHIPS COULD SHELTER THERE IN THE SHADE. AND IN THIS WONDERFUL WOOD LIVED A NIGHTINGALE WHICH SANG SO DELICIOUSLY THAT ALL WHO HEARD IT STOOD ROOTED TO THE SPOT. NEVER HAD SUCH MUSIC BEEN HEARD BEFORE IN ANY WOOD IN THE WORLD. EVEN THE POOR FISHERMAN, BUSY WITH HIS NETS IN THE BAY, WOULD PAUSE IN HIS WORK TO LISTEN. 'HEAVENS, HOW BEAUTIFUL THAT SONG IS!' HE WOULD SAY; AND, NIGHT AFTER NIGHT, WHEN THE BIRD SANG HE WOULD FORGET HIS TOIL TO MURMUR, 'HOW BEAUTIFUL! HOW BEAUTIFUL!'

— THE NIGHTINGALE
AFTER A FAIRY TALE BY
HANS CHRISTIAN ANDERSEN

EMPIRE STATE BUILDING 1980

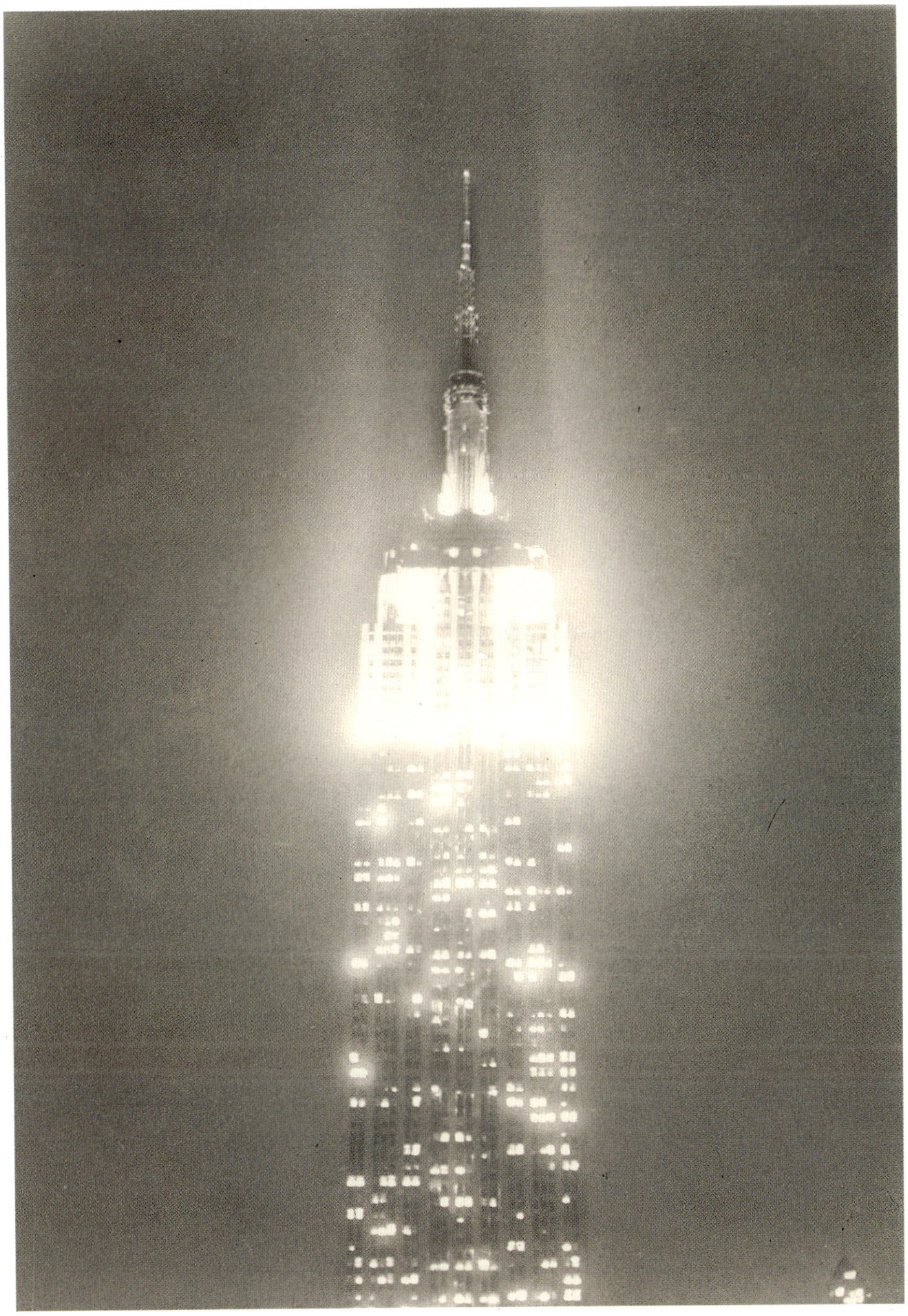

TULIP, MUSIC 1977

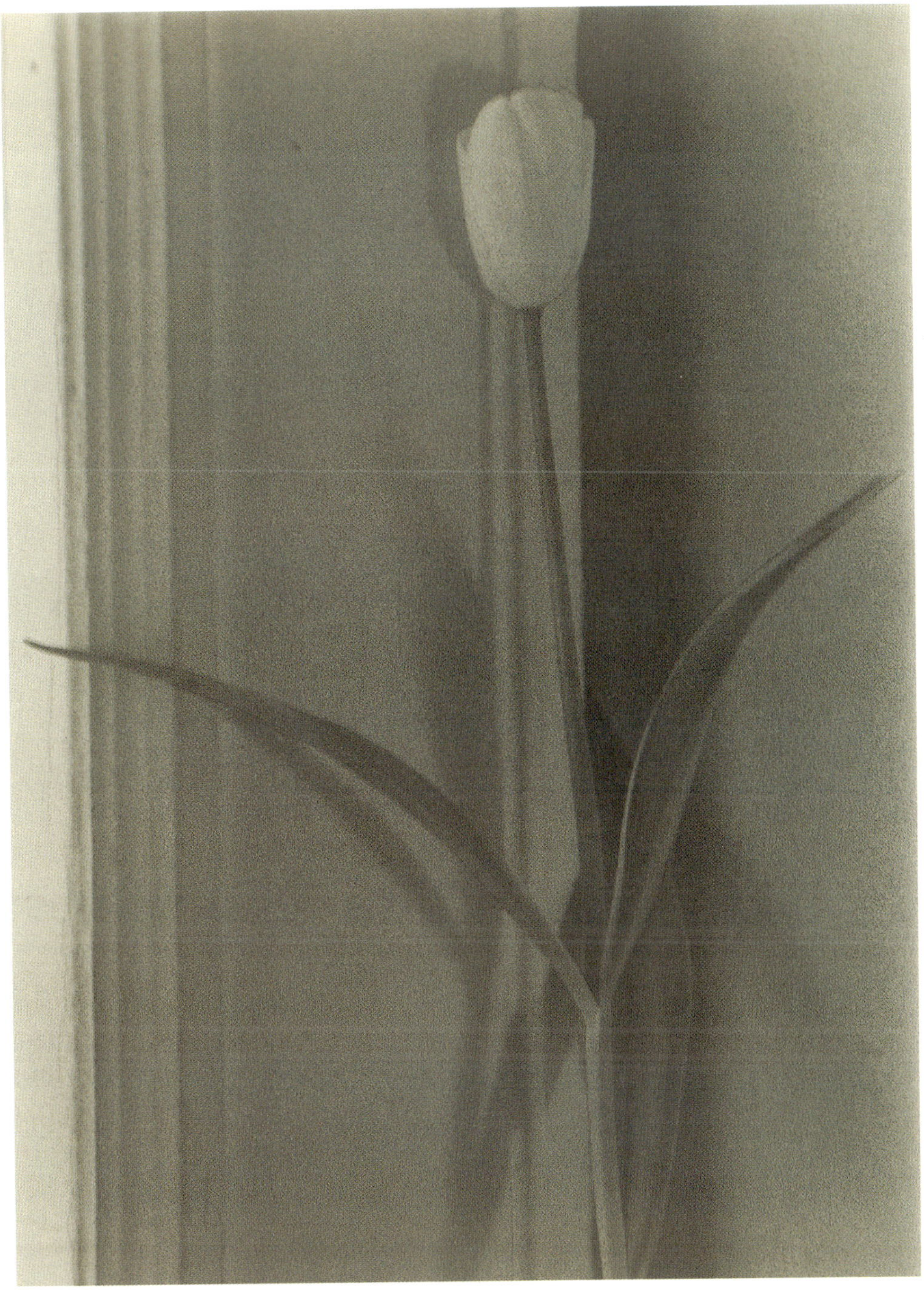

GREY MODERN VASE, MAGRITTE ROCK 1977

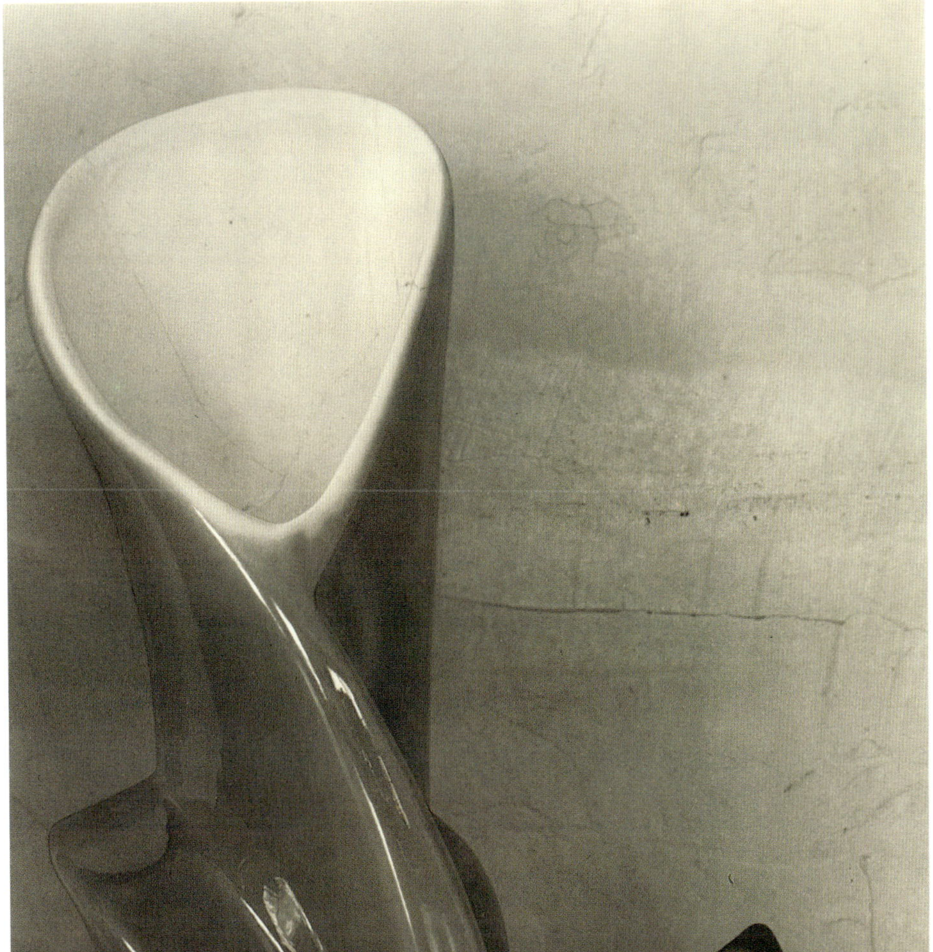

JACK IN THE PULPIT 1978

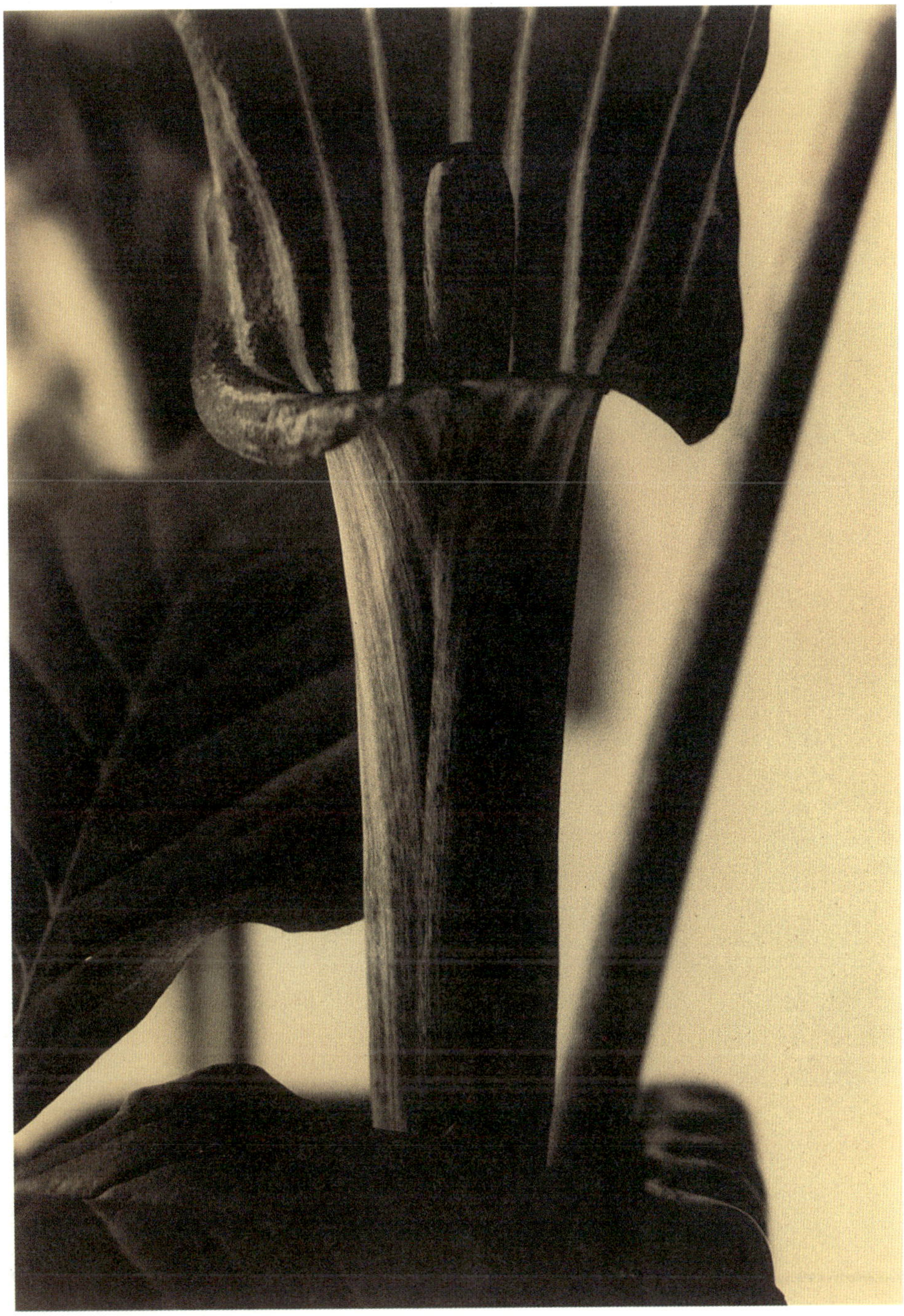

EVYAN 1975

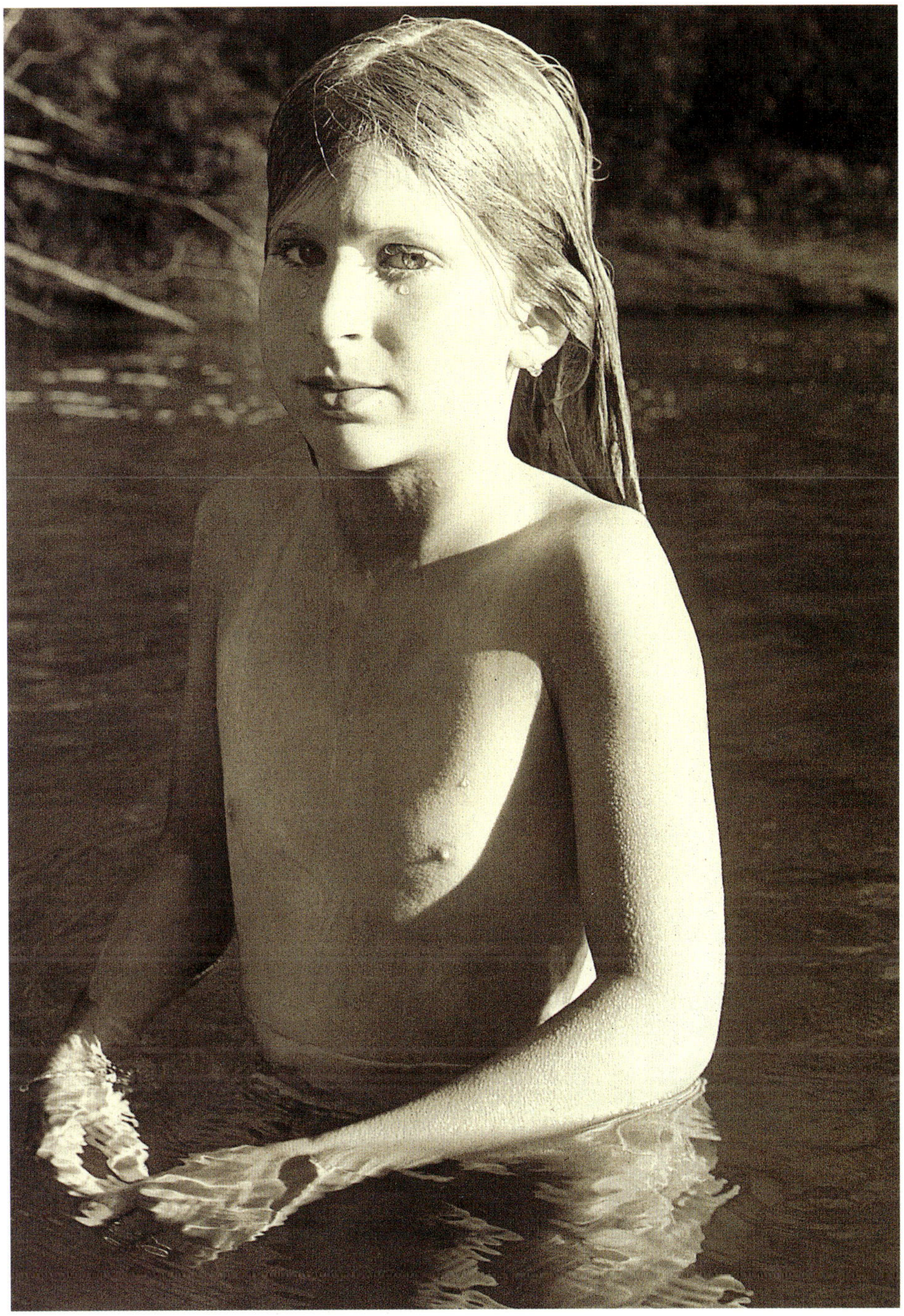

WHITE TRUNK, SYCAMORE 1977

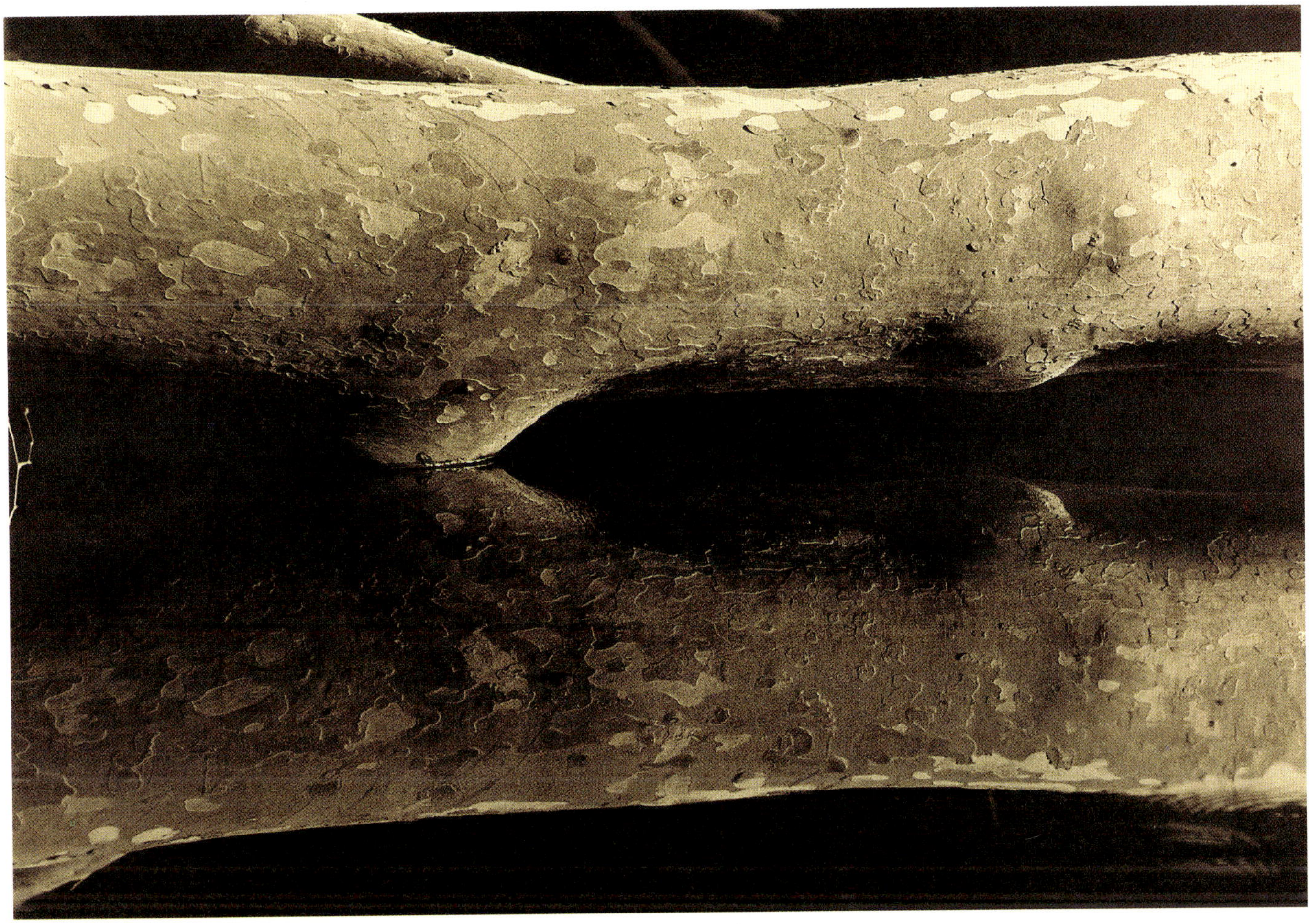

BEGA, CHATHAM 1977

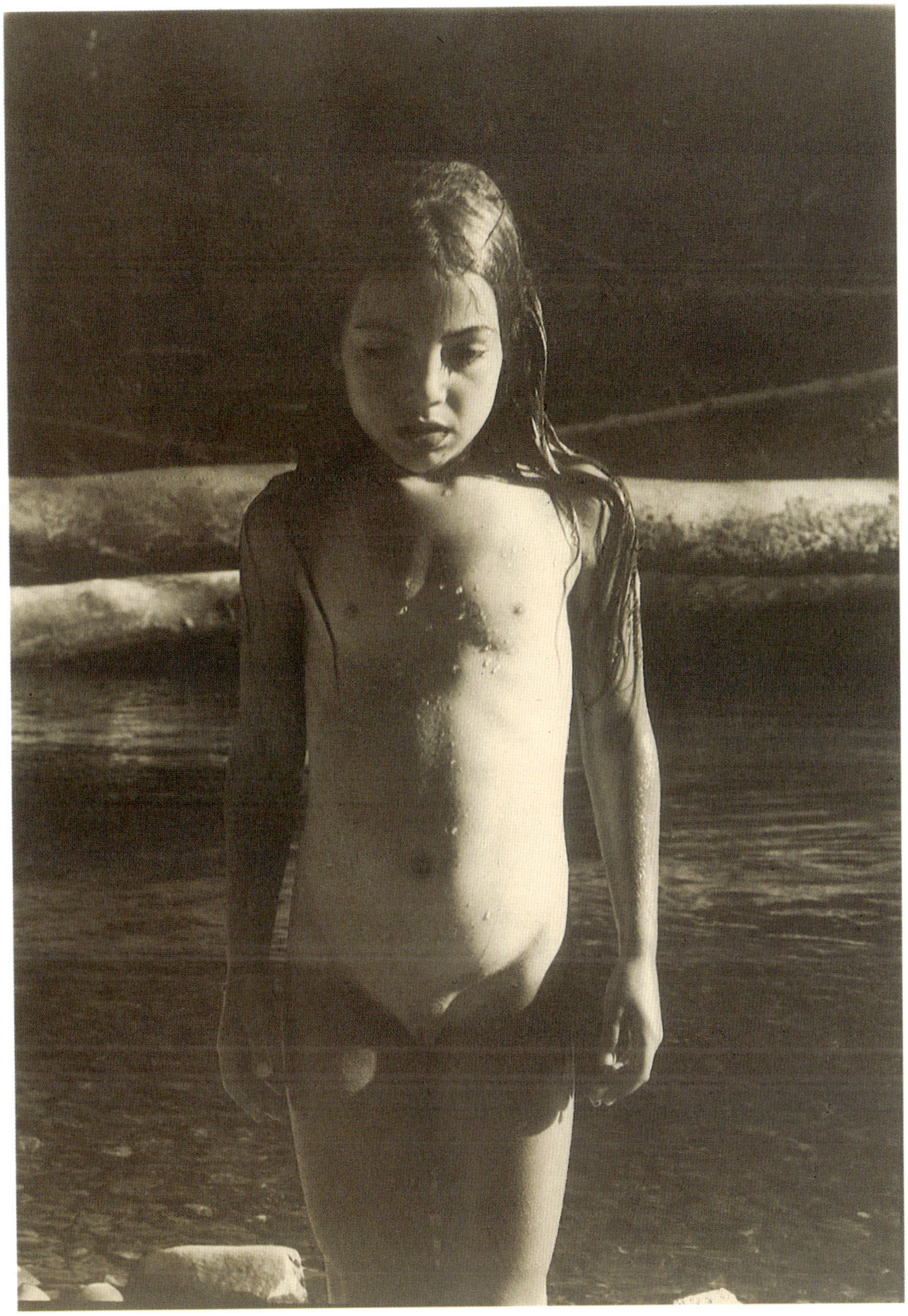

JEFFREY, STELLA FEVER 1978

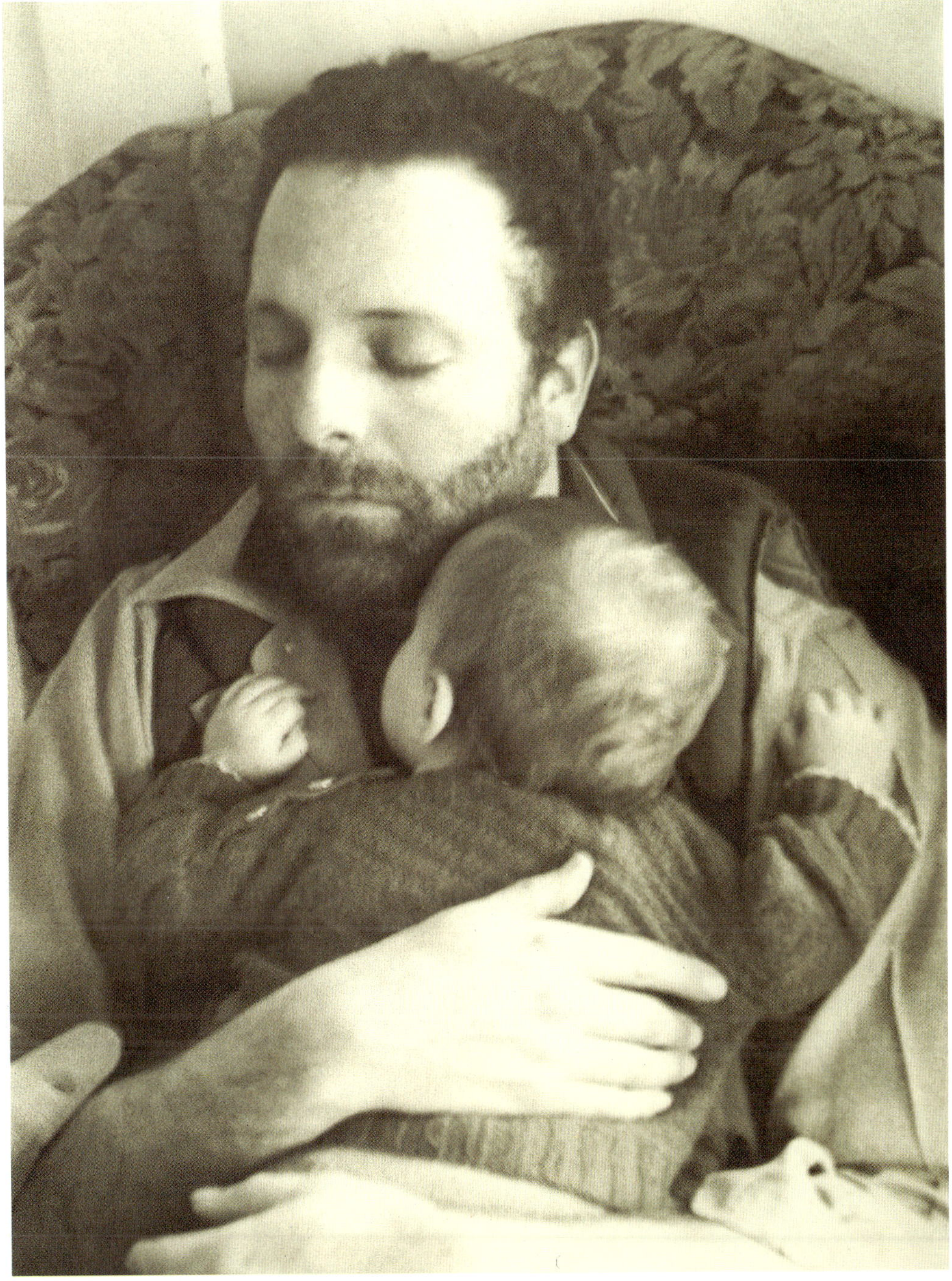

ANTARCTICA 1977

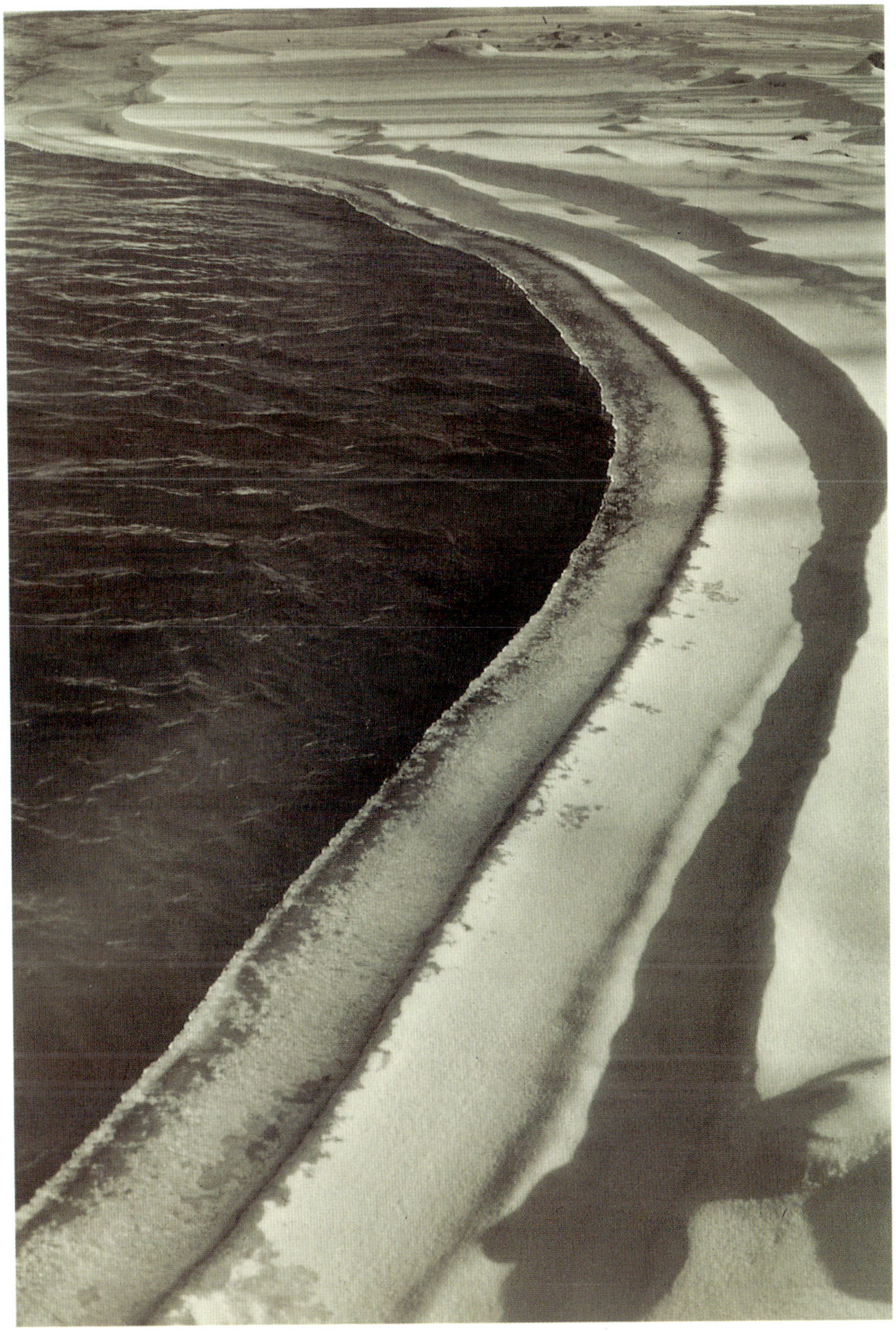

EVYAN 1974

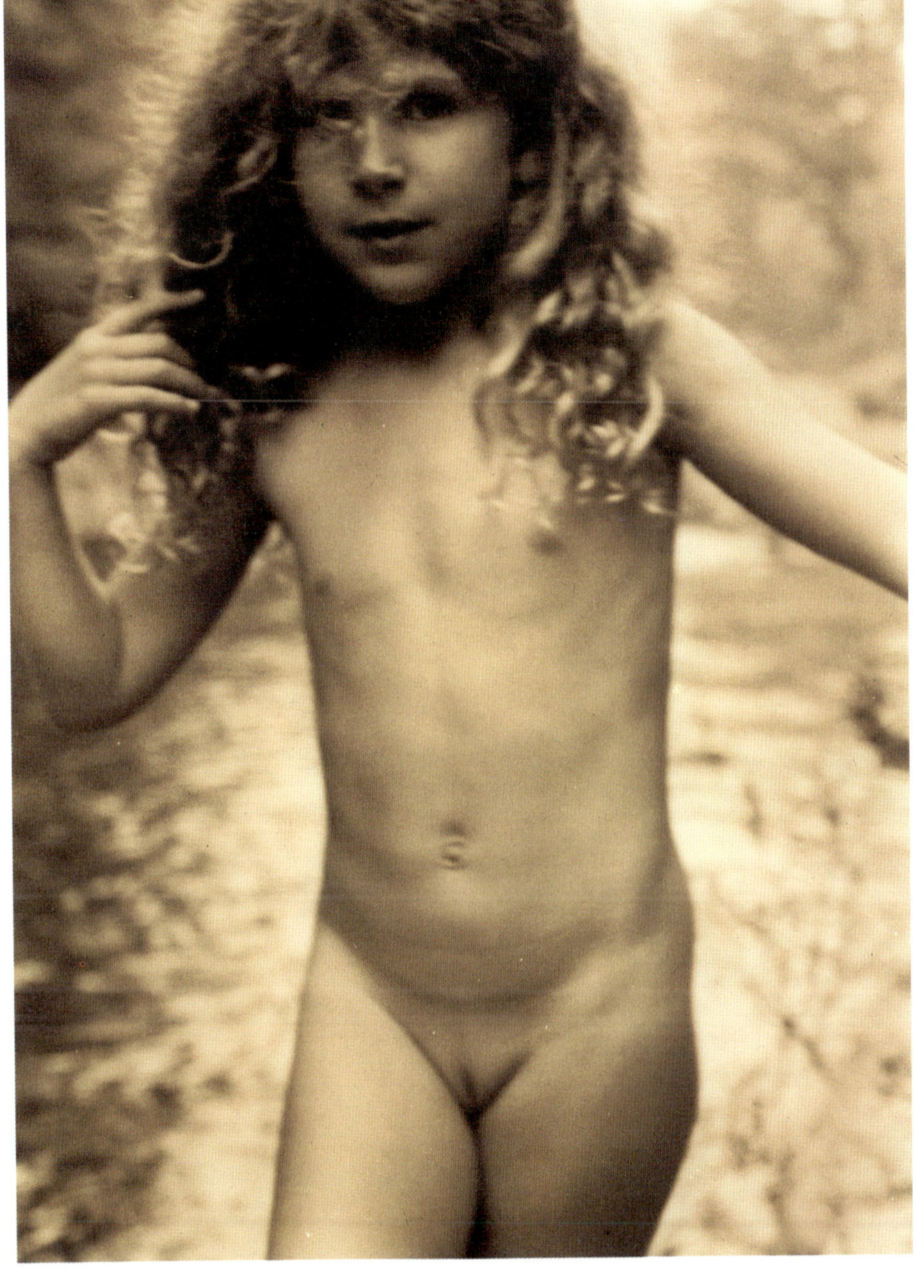

CHILDREN ASLEEP 1977

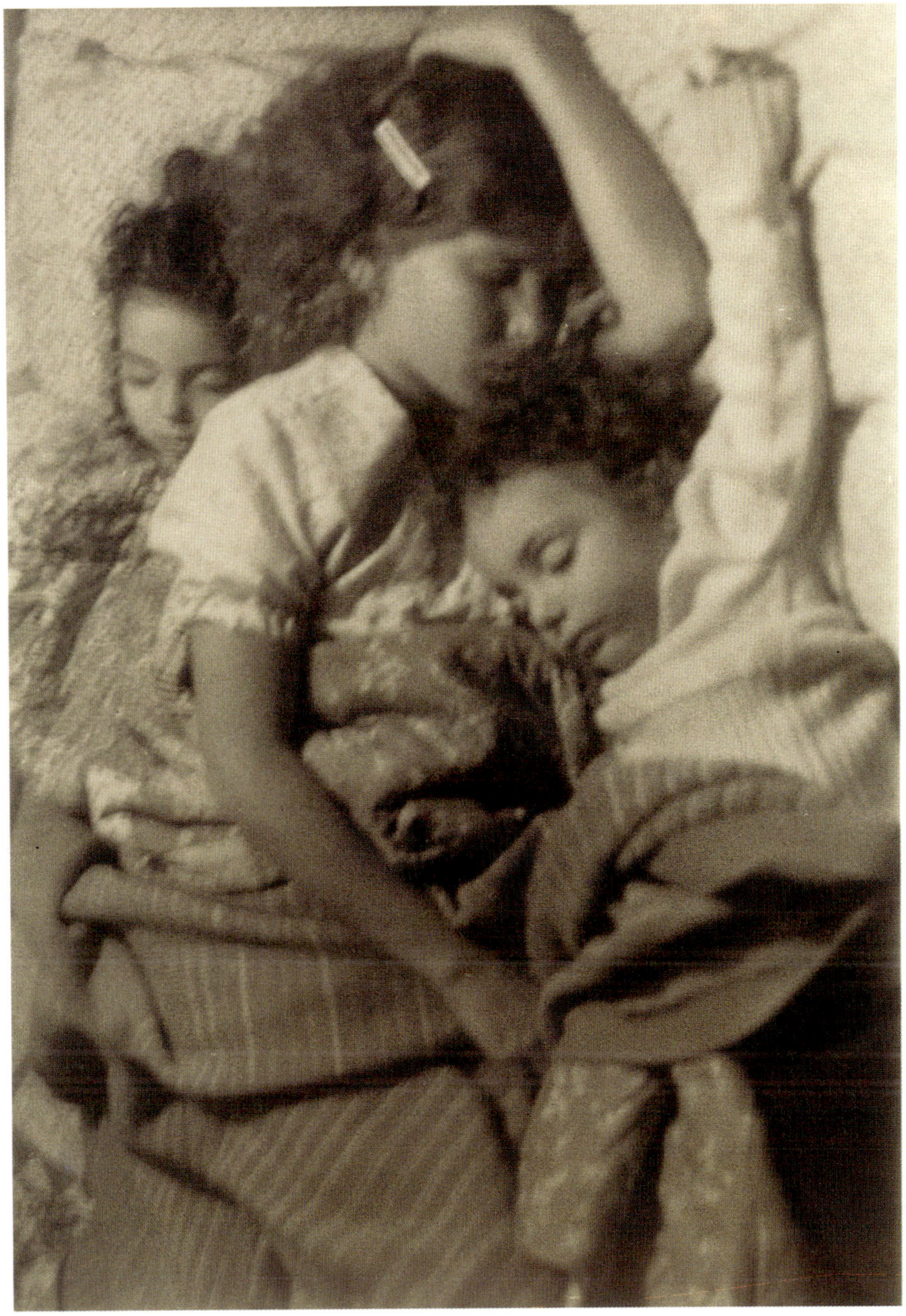

BEGA, FAN 1977

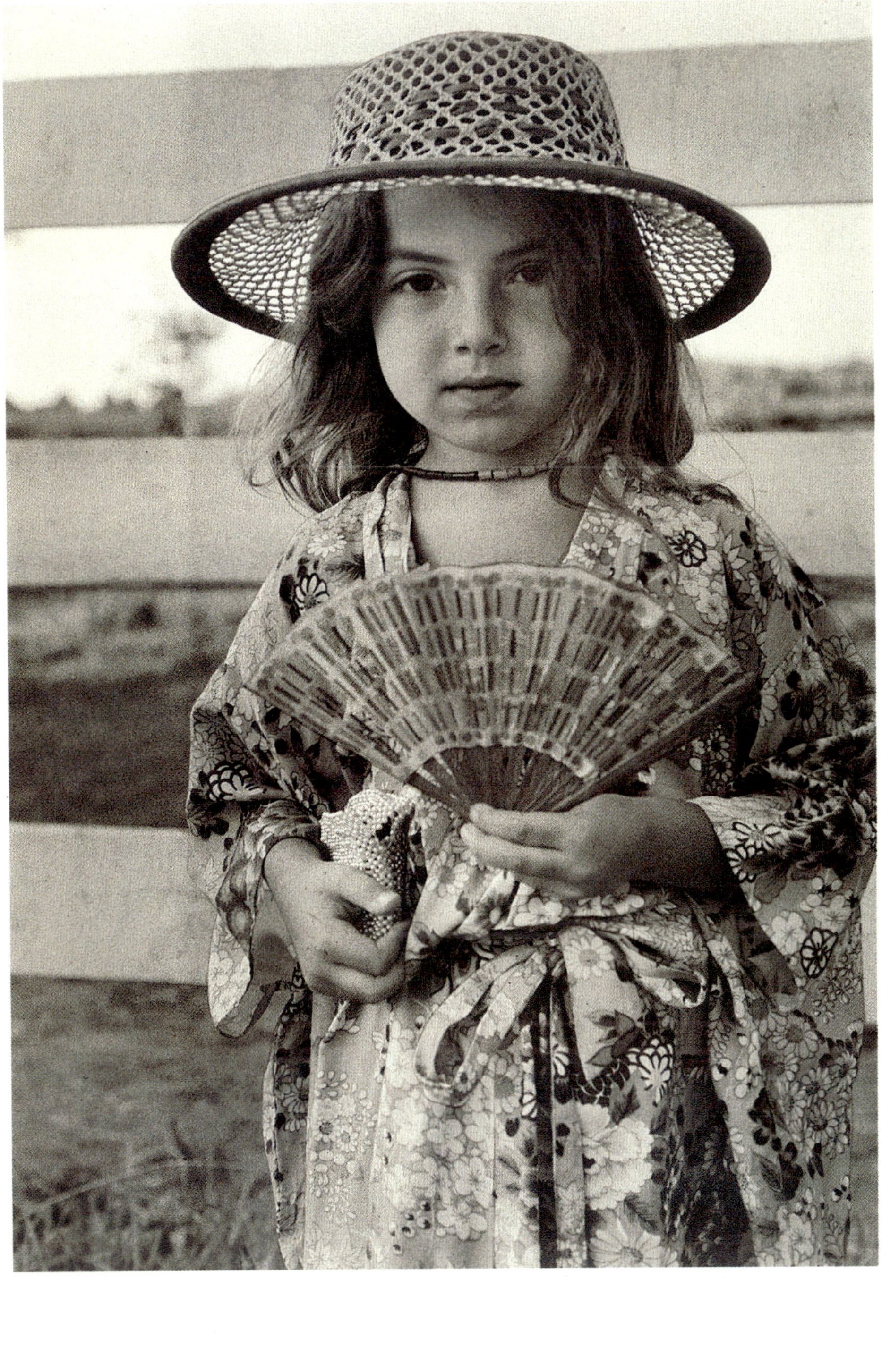

BEGA, ASLEEP ON THE RED LOVE SEAT 1977

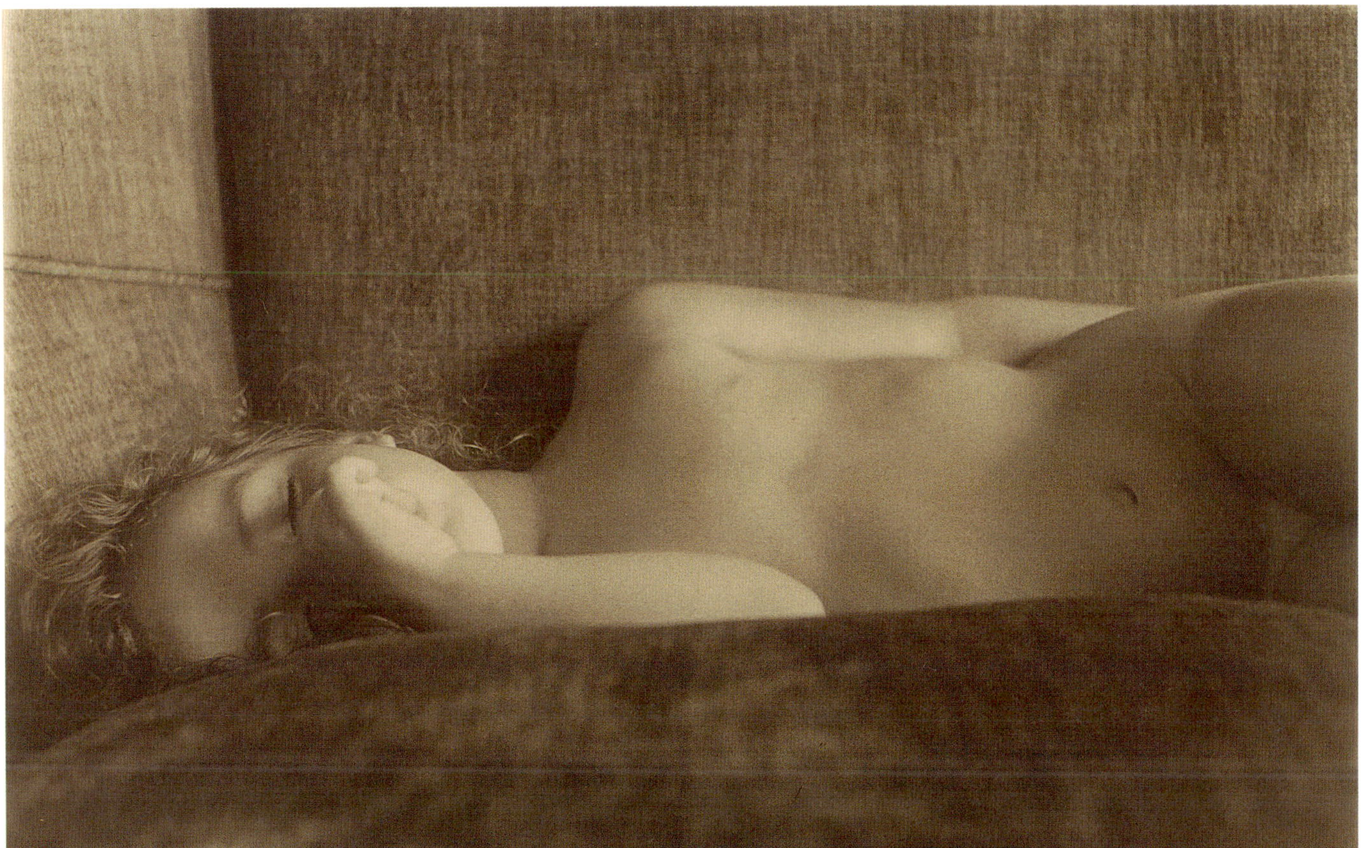

BEGA, KINDERHOOK CREEK 1977

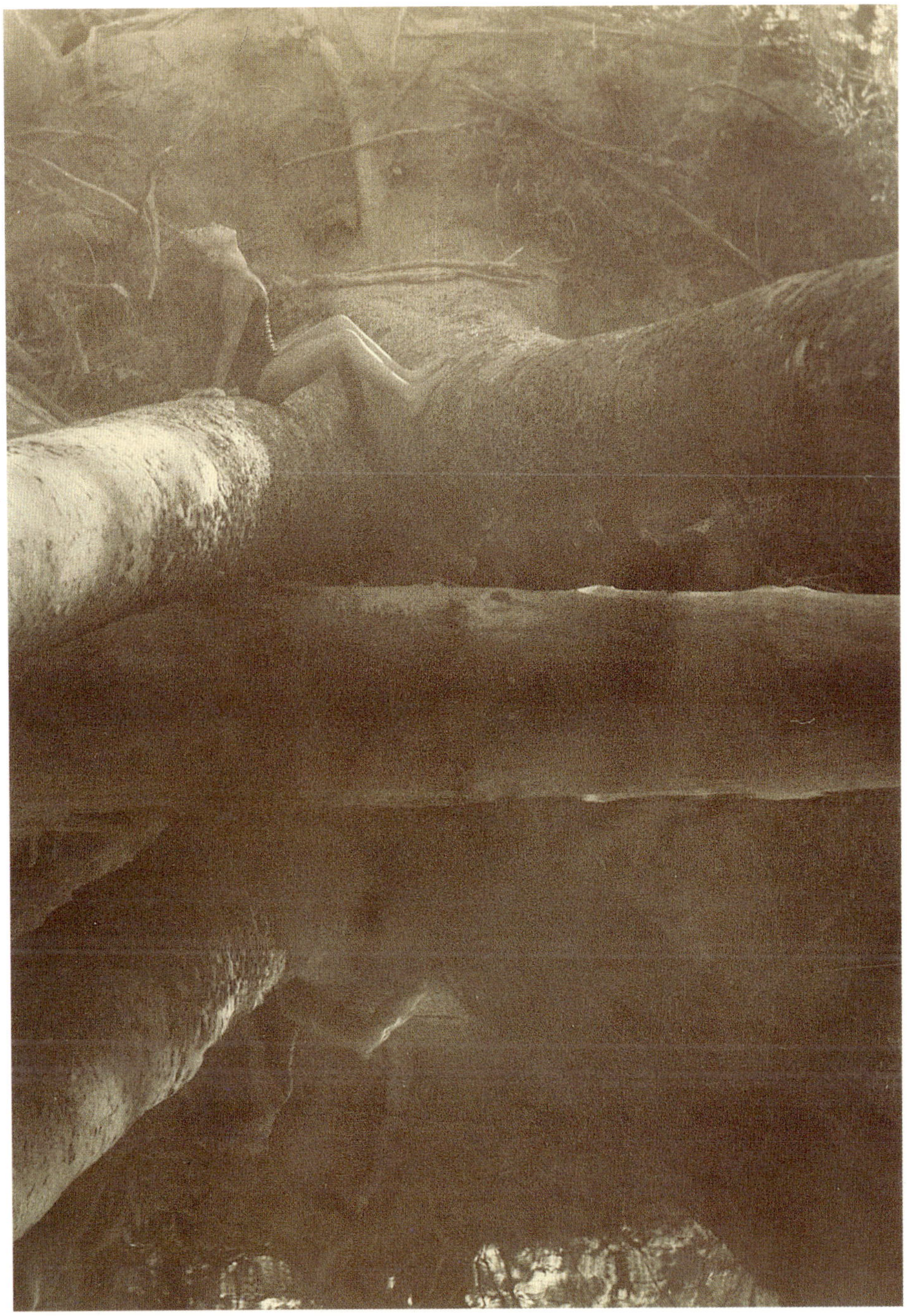

WHITE VASE, WHITE CALLA 1977

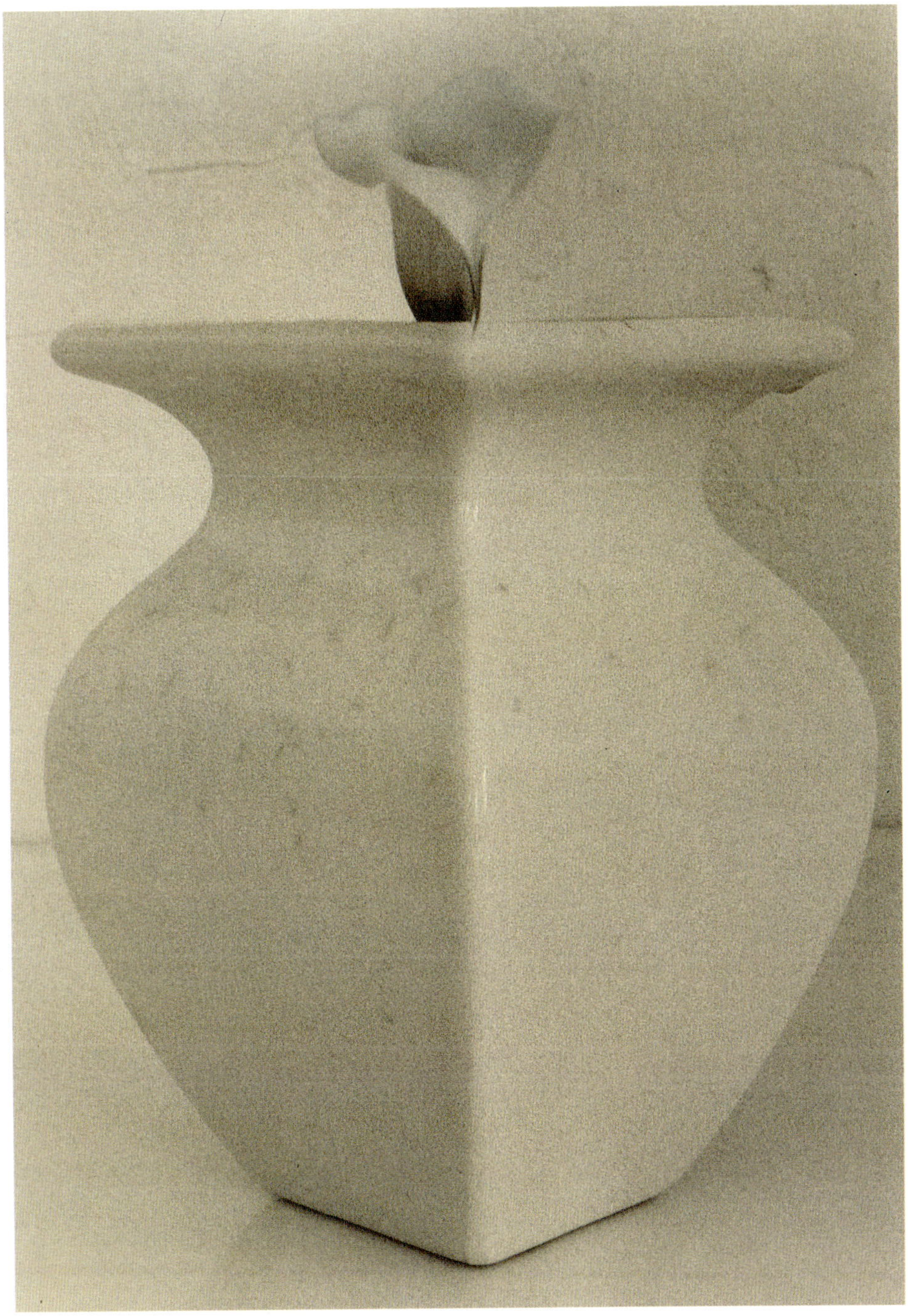

RUBY 1978

RUBY 1978

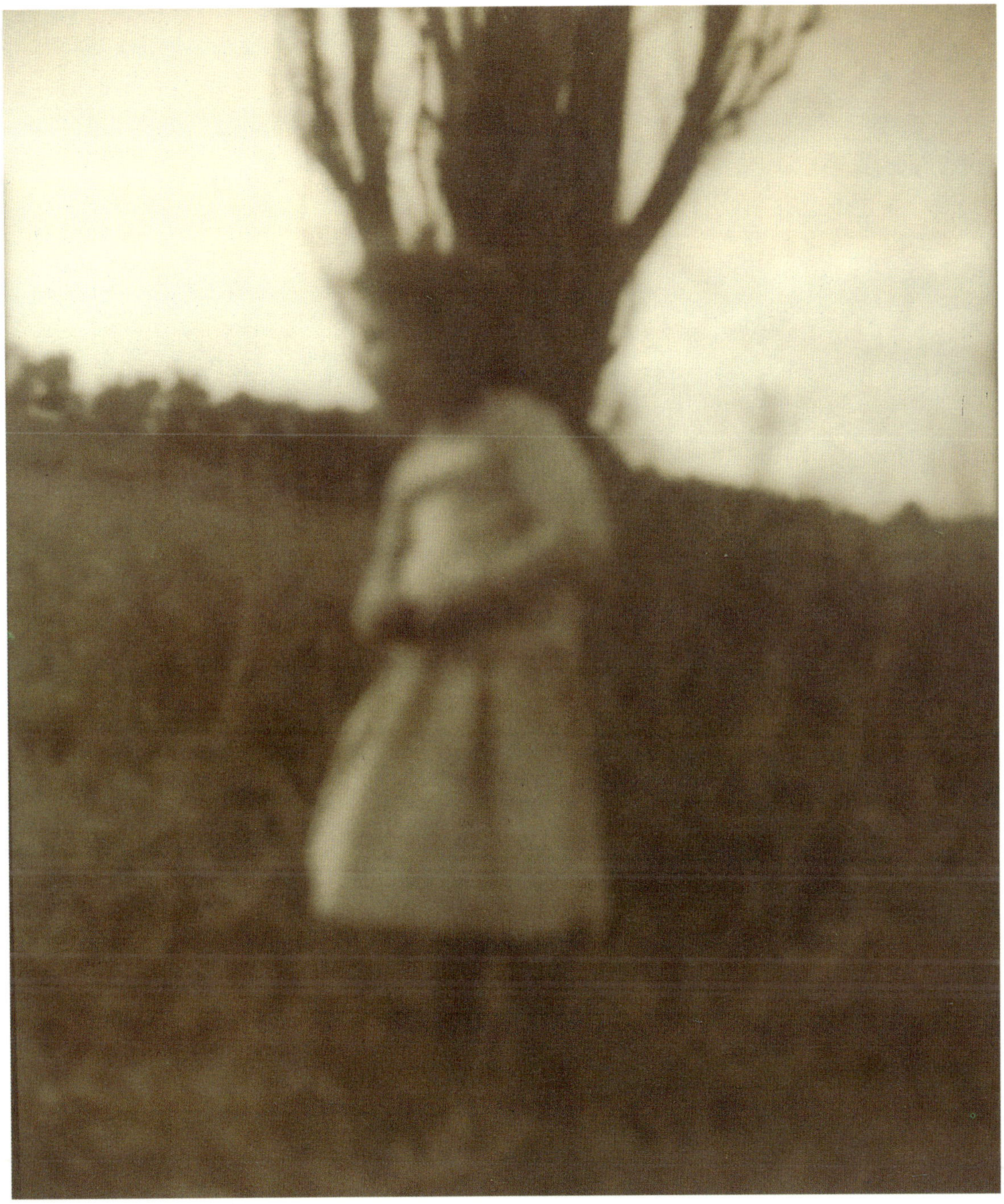

TULIP 1977

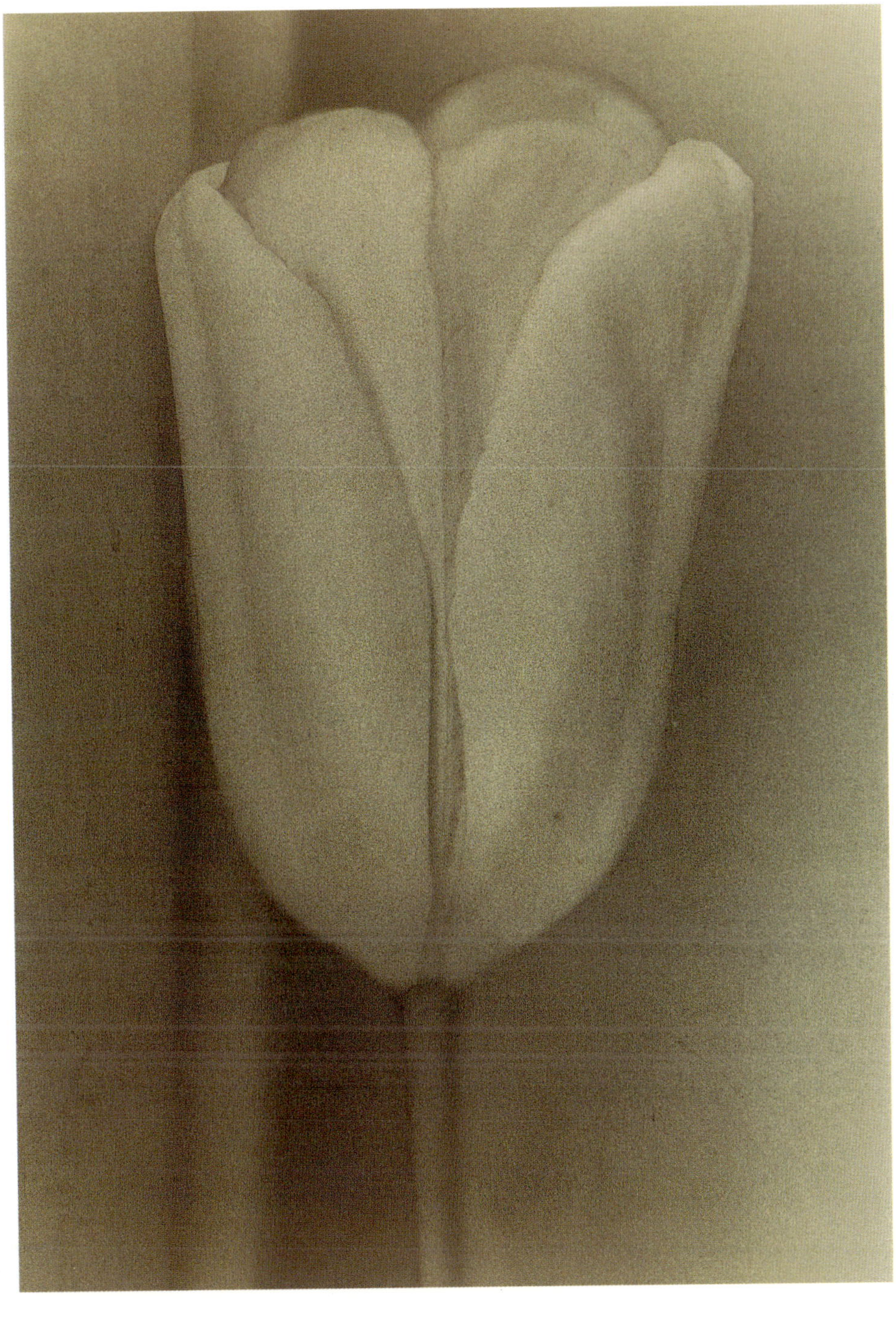

GREY VASE, VANDA ORCHID 1980

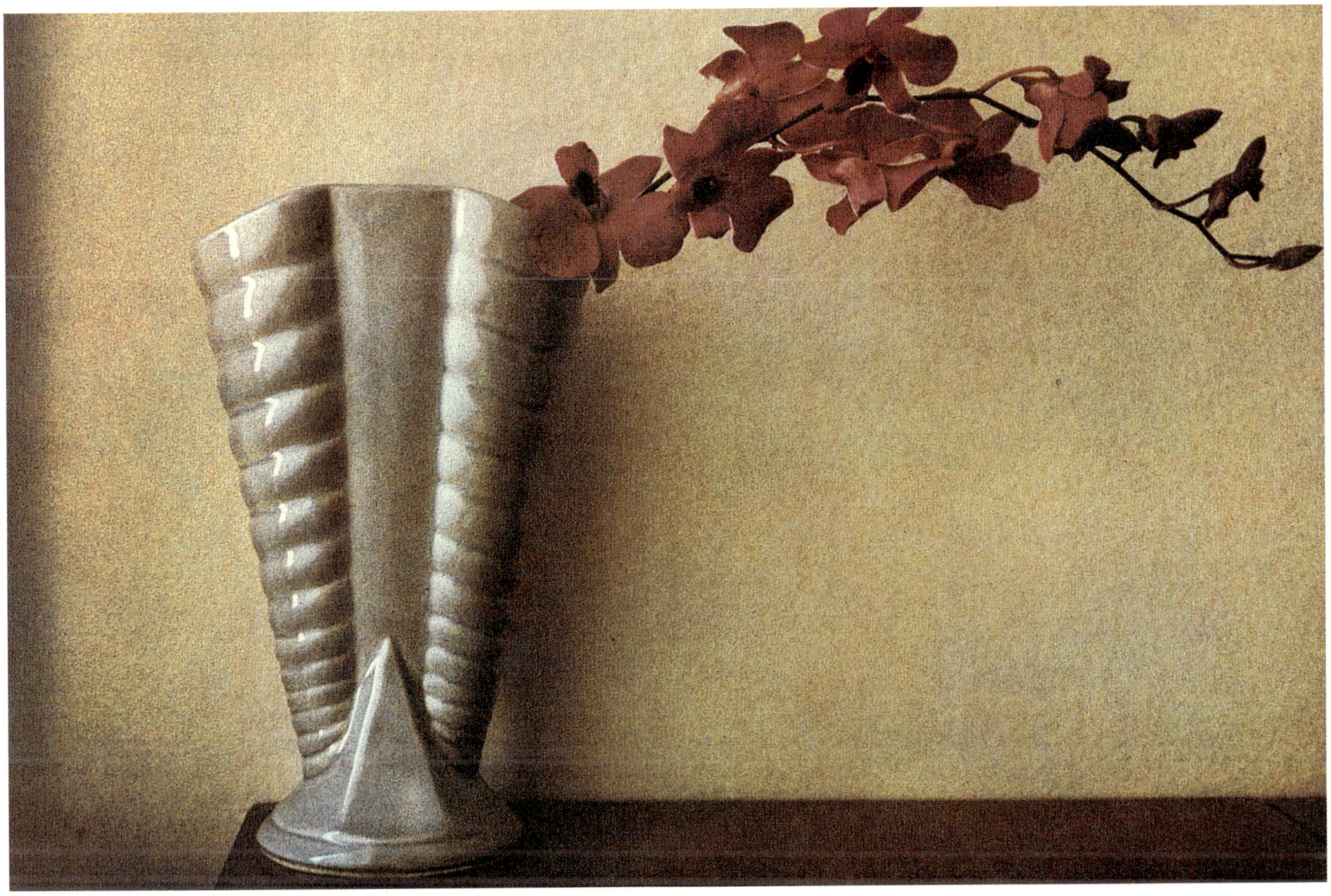

JOHN, TORSO 1980

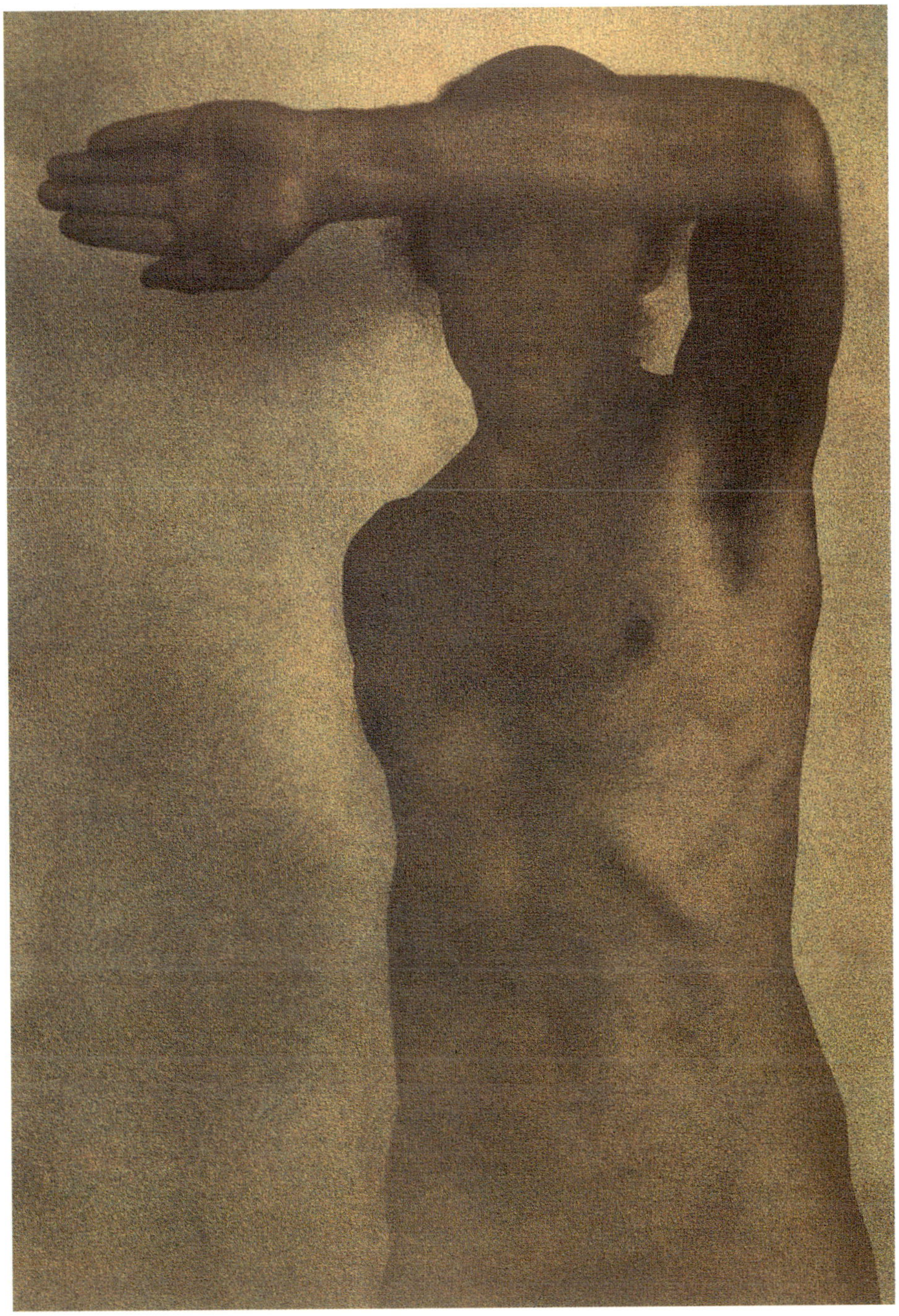

THREE PLUMS 1981

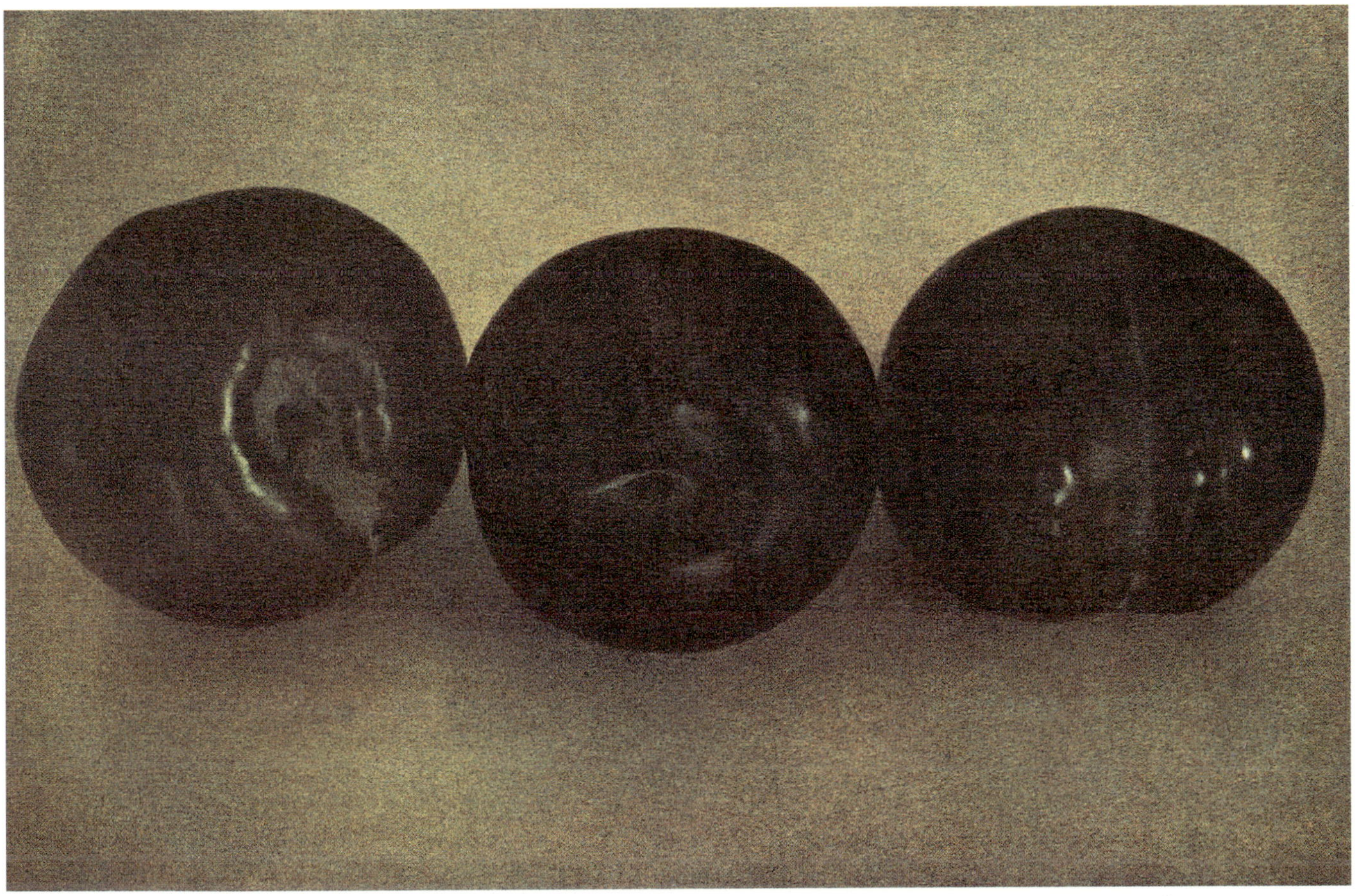

STELLA, GALAXY 1982

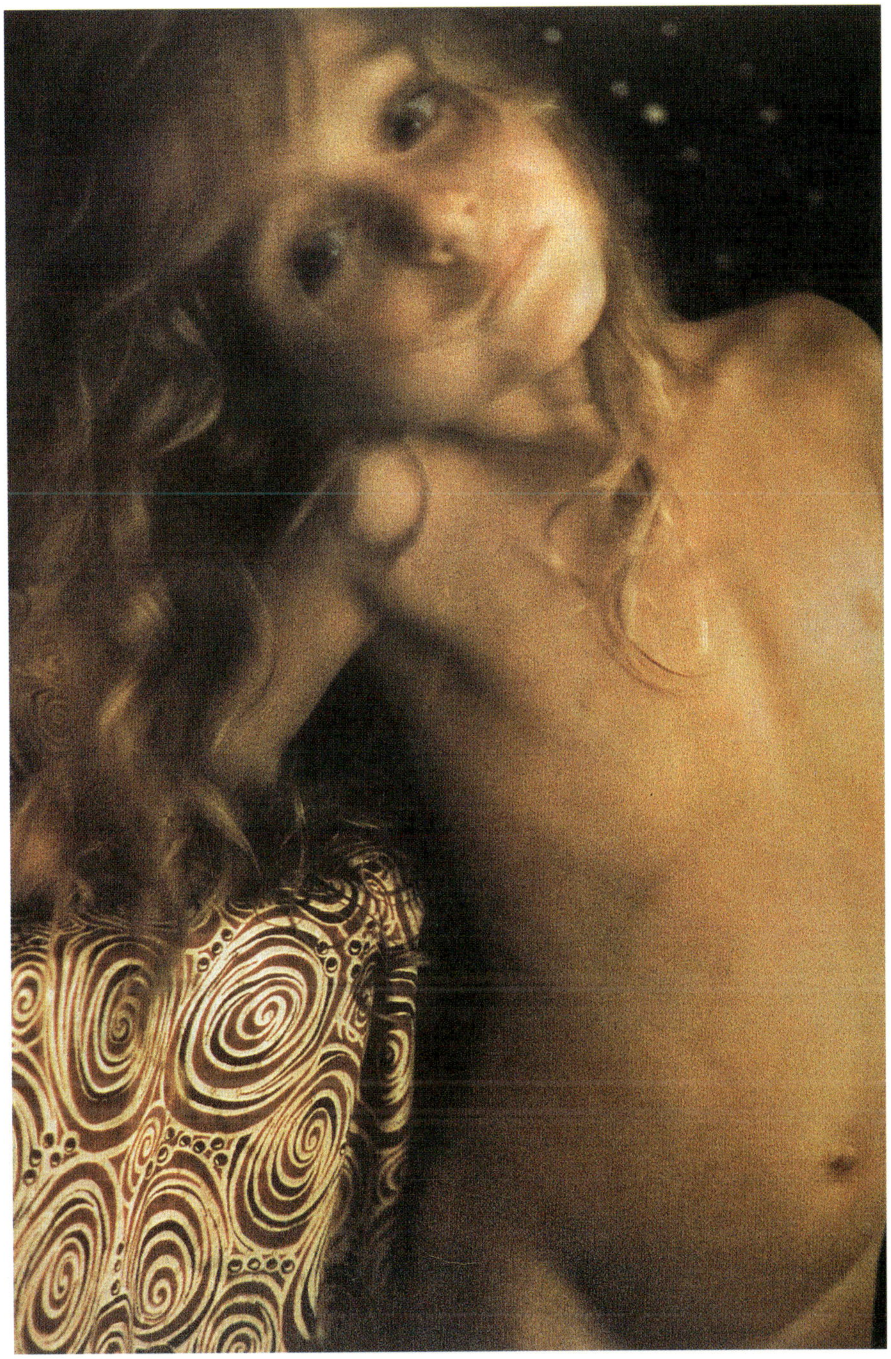

LISA, RED JUMPSUIT 1980

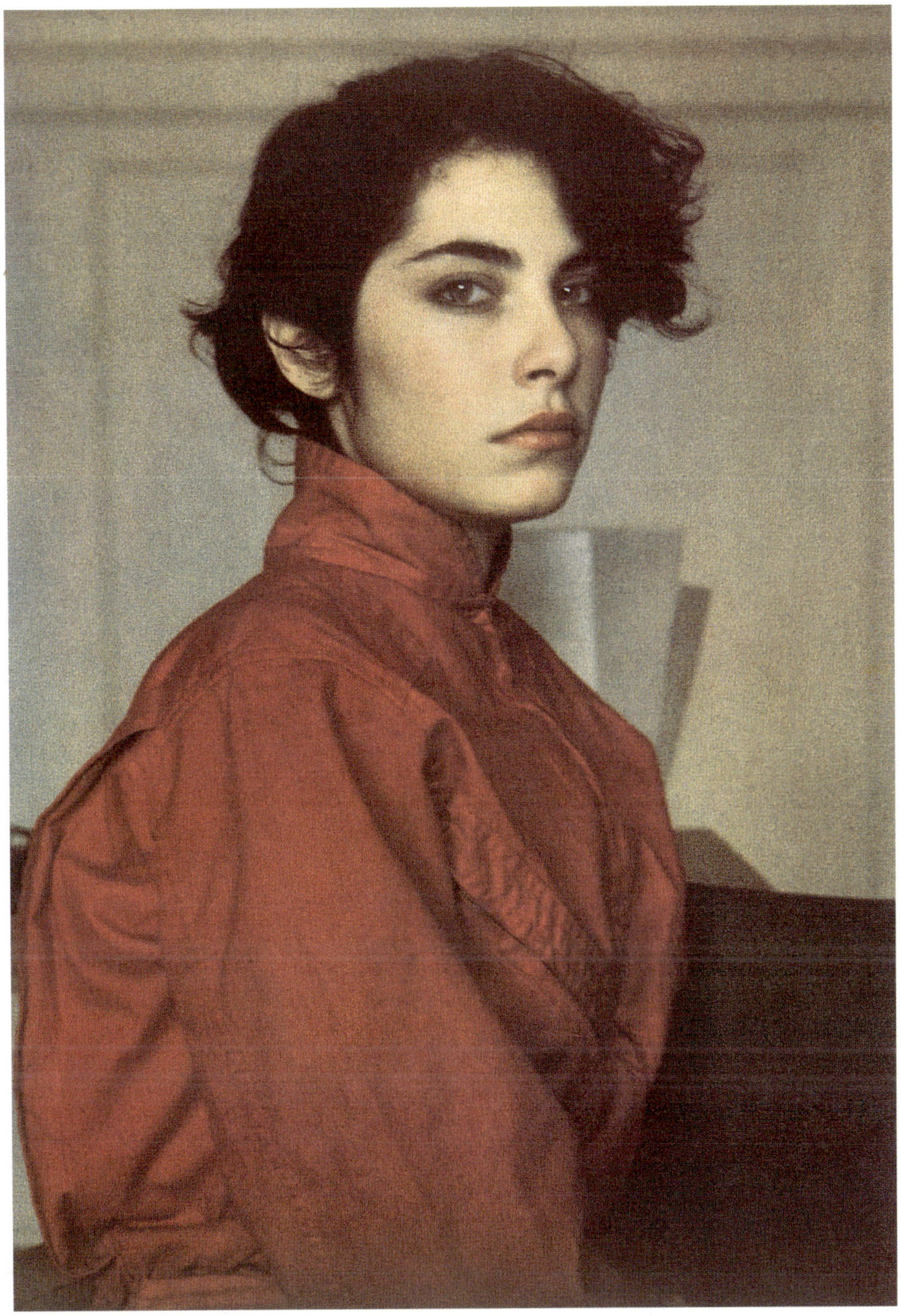

RUBY, MIAMI SHIRT 1980

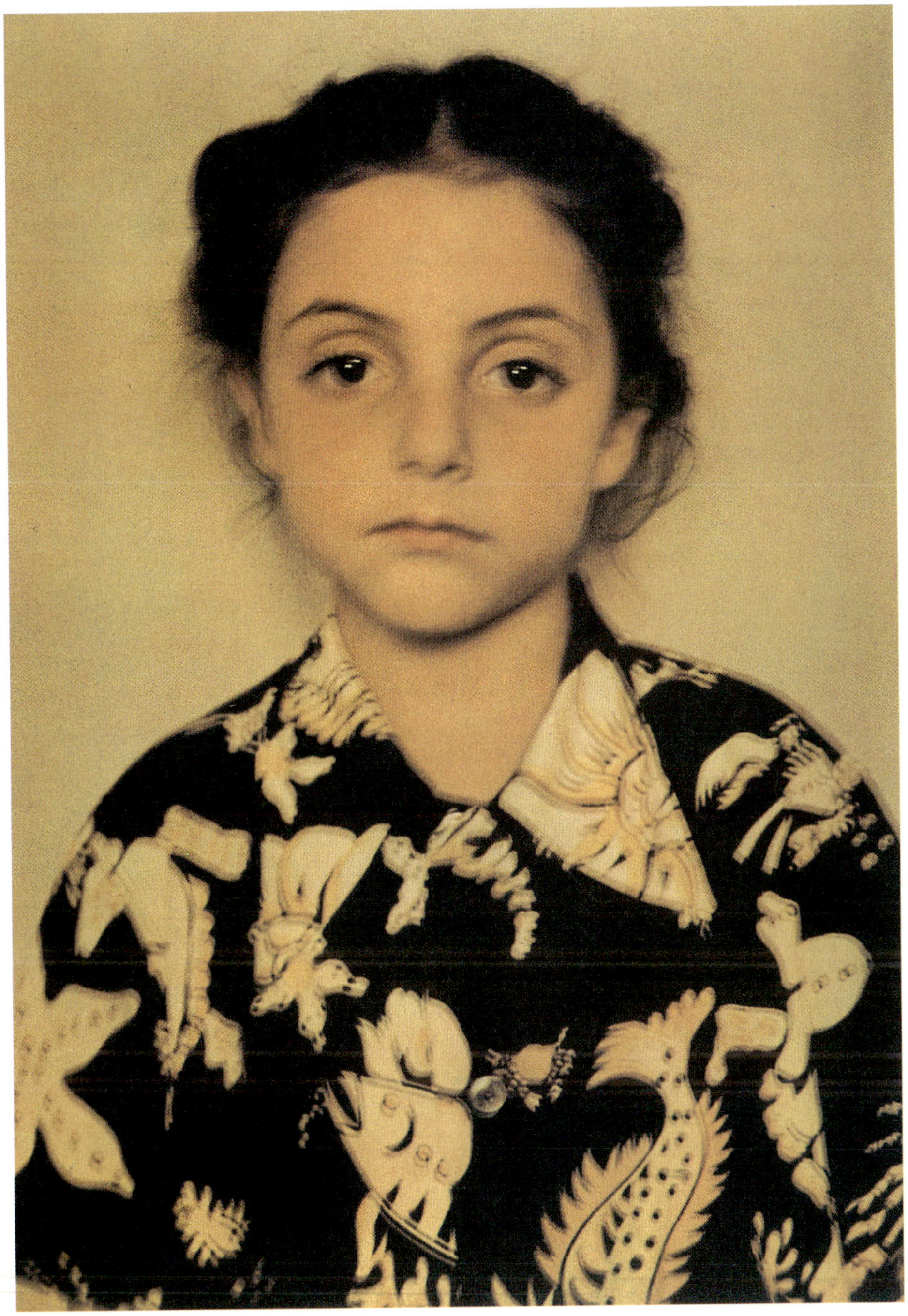

STILL LIFE 1979

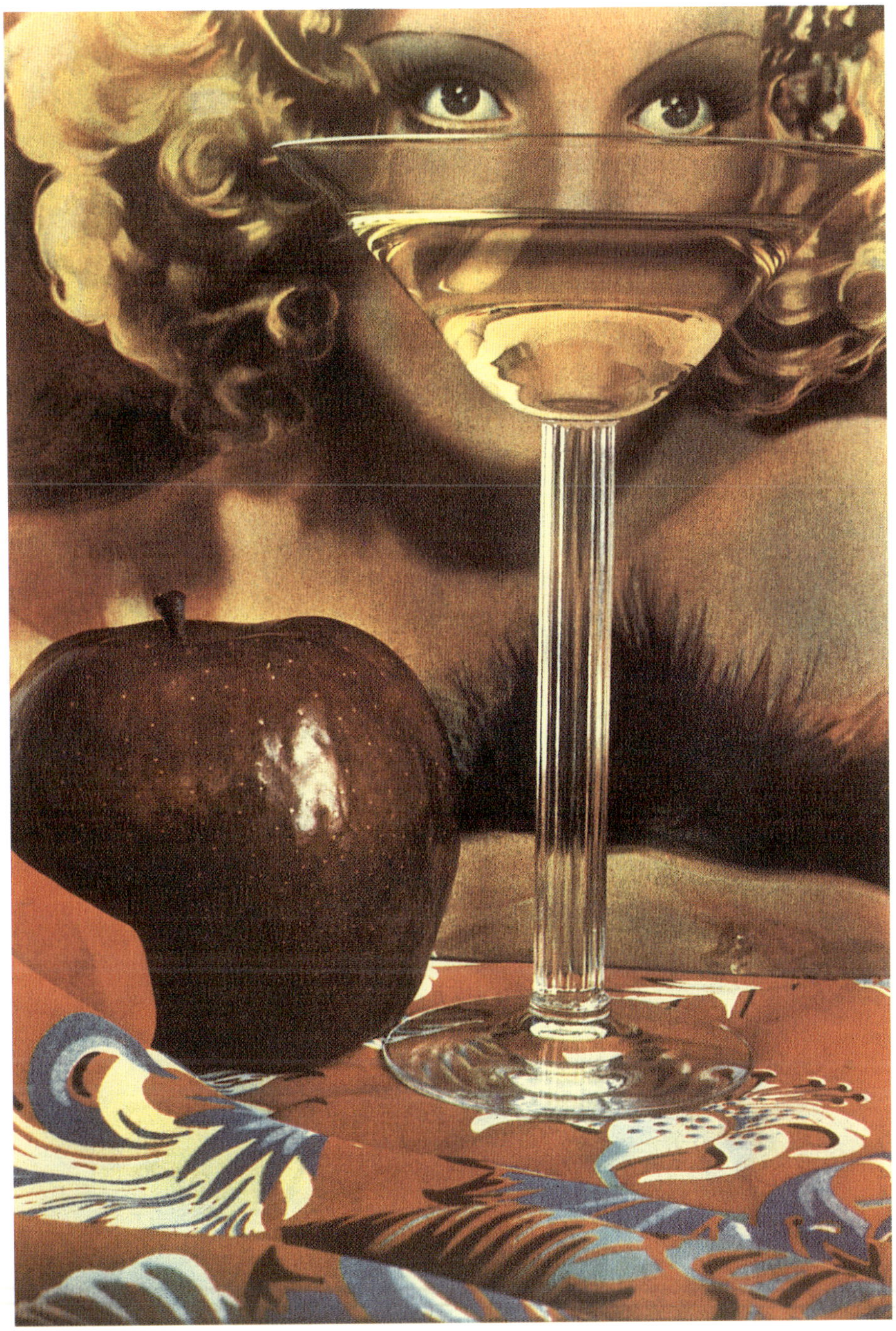

MICHAL, DREAM 1980

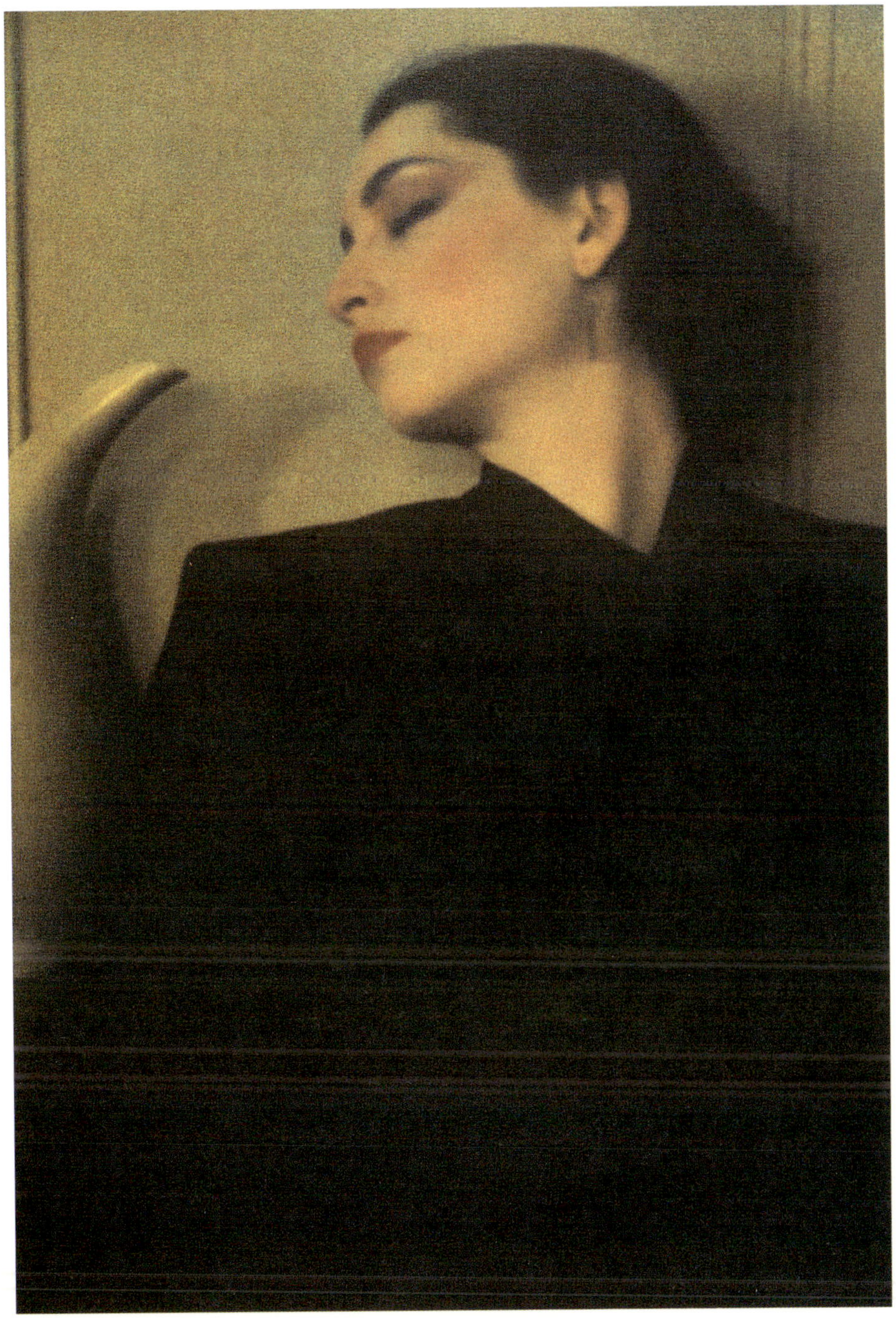

CALLA 1980

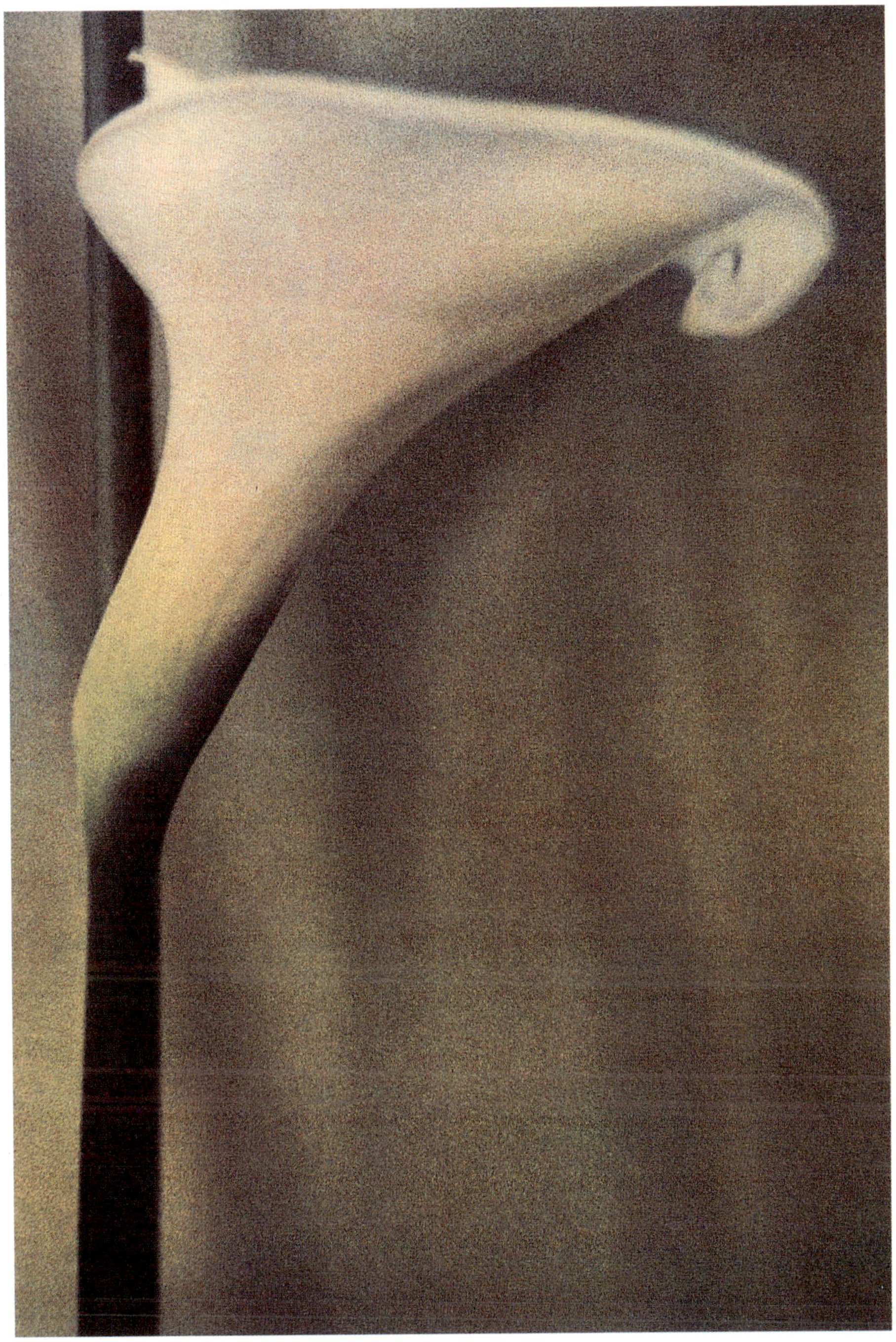

MICHAL, MERMAID 1980

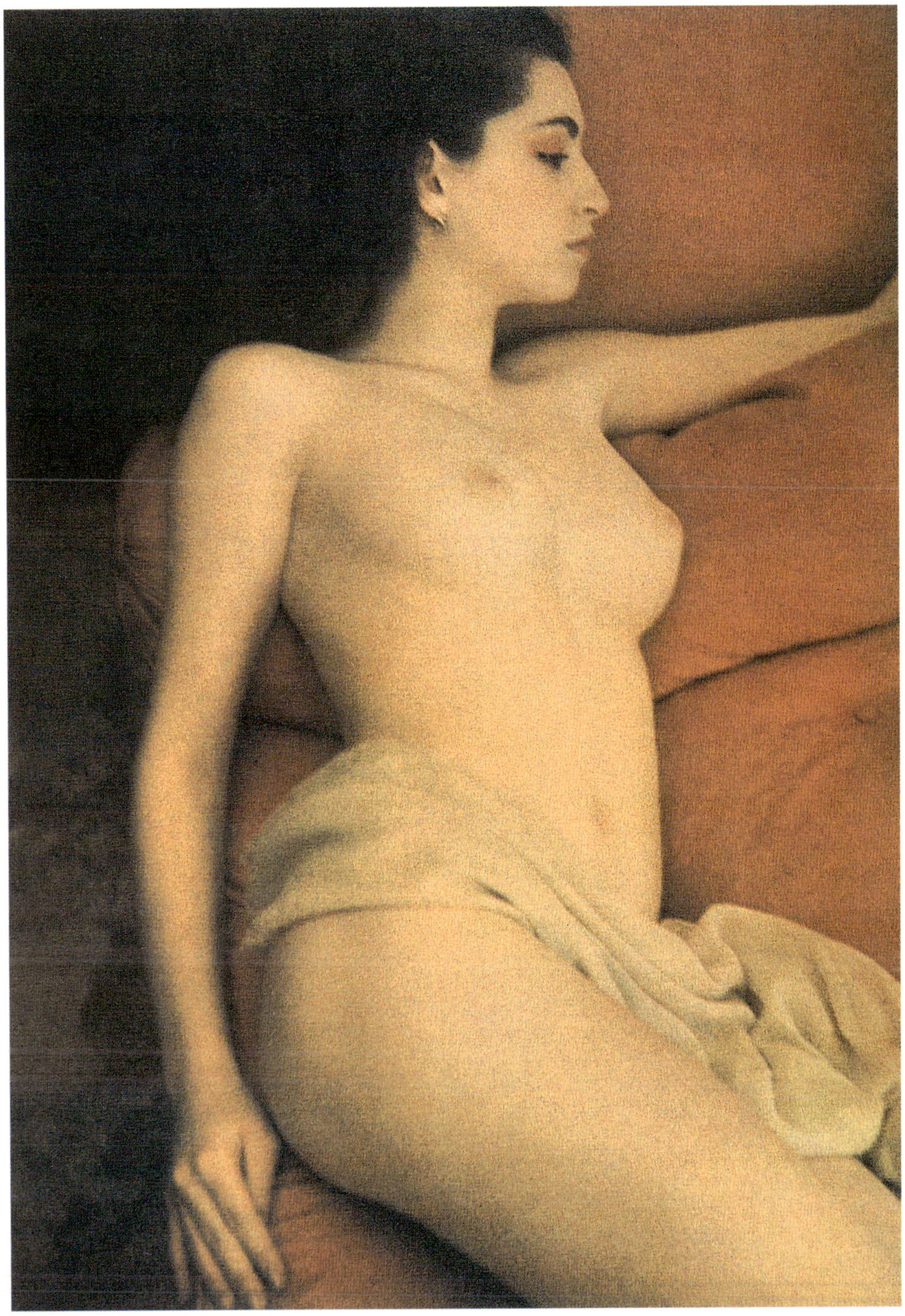

BEGA, STILL LIFE WITH PEPPERS 1982

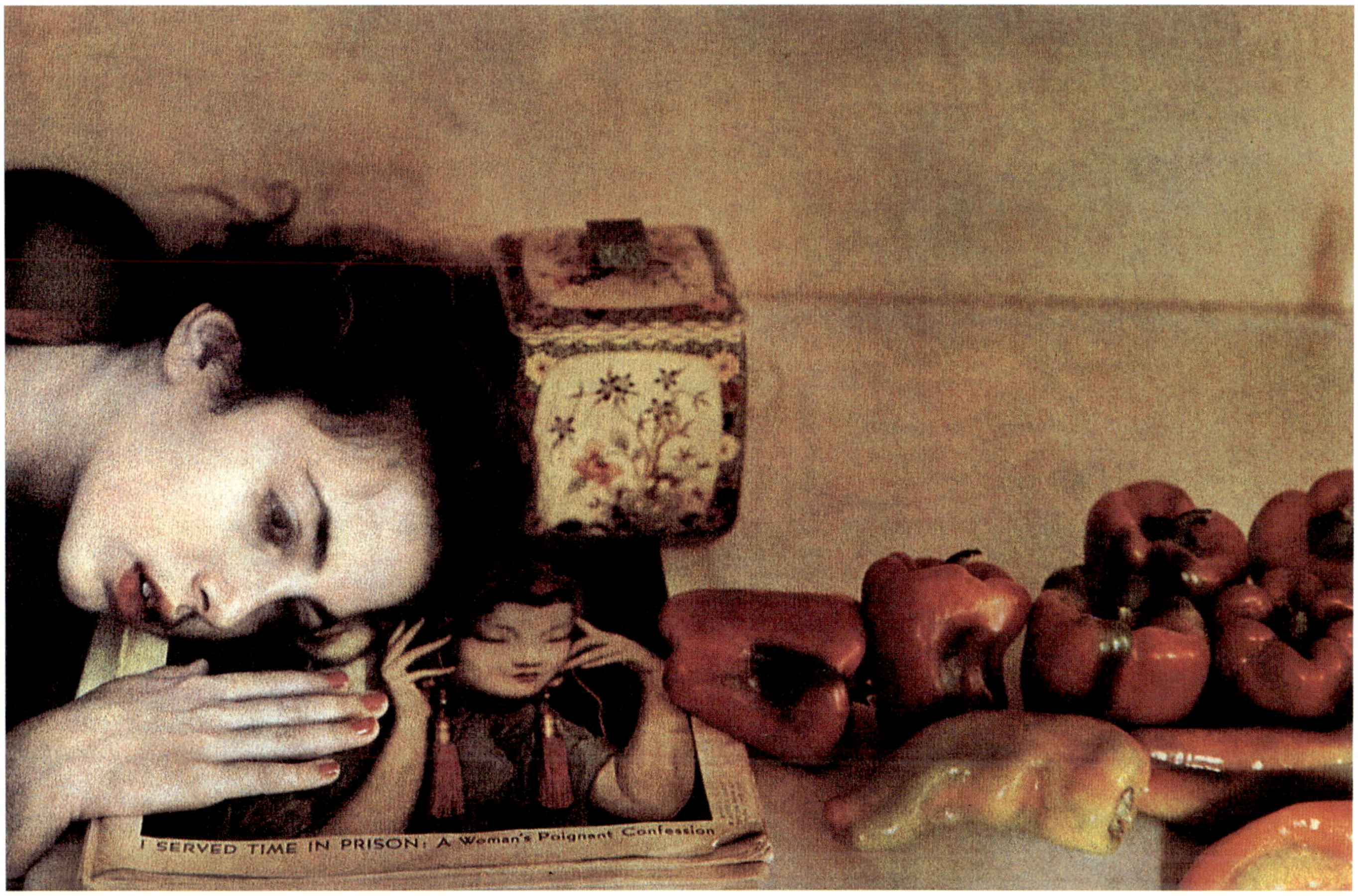
I SERVED TIME IN PRISON: A Woman's Poignant Confession

BEGA, PLASTIC HAT 1983

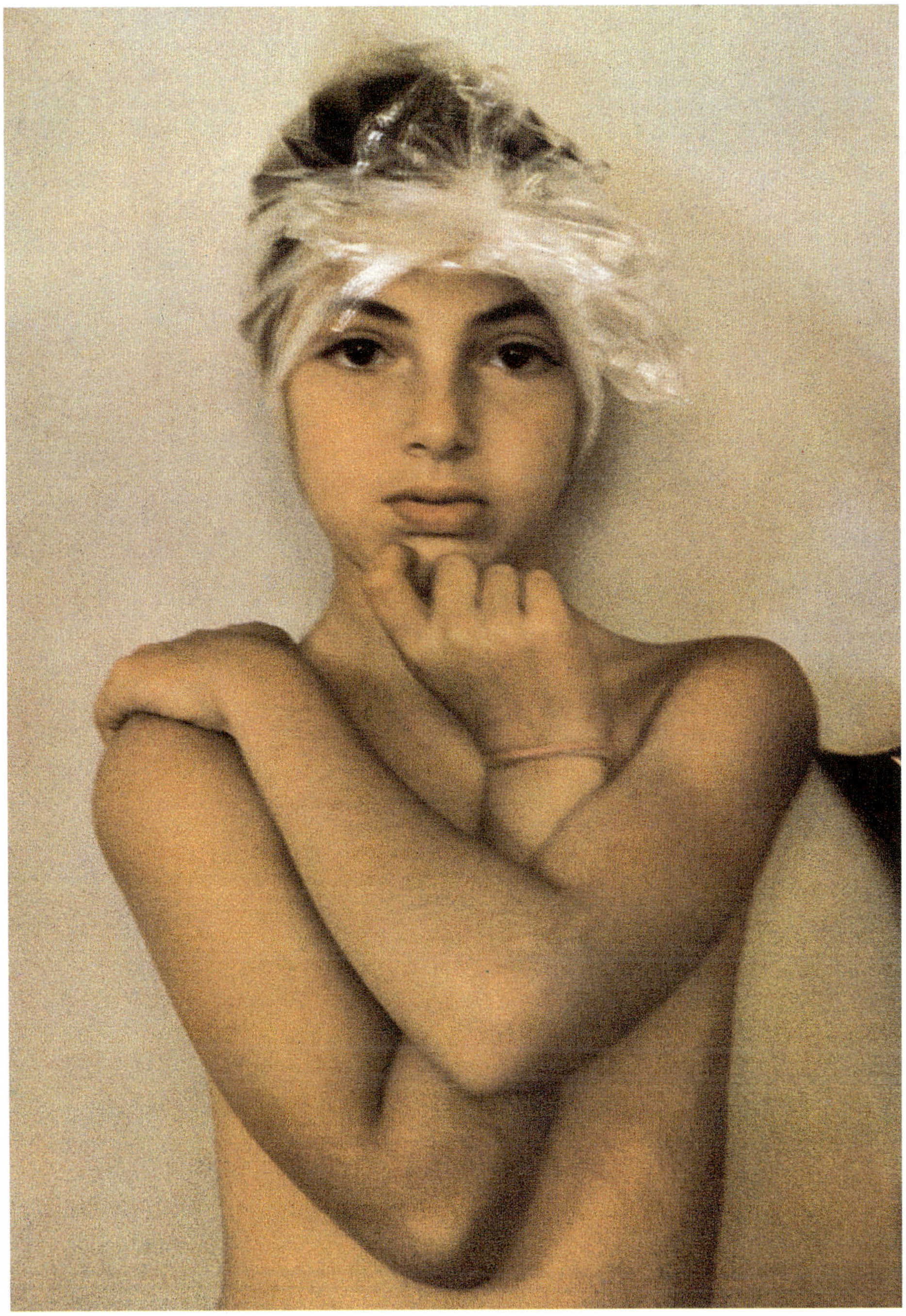

HOMAGE TO MAN RAY 1983

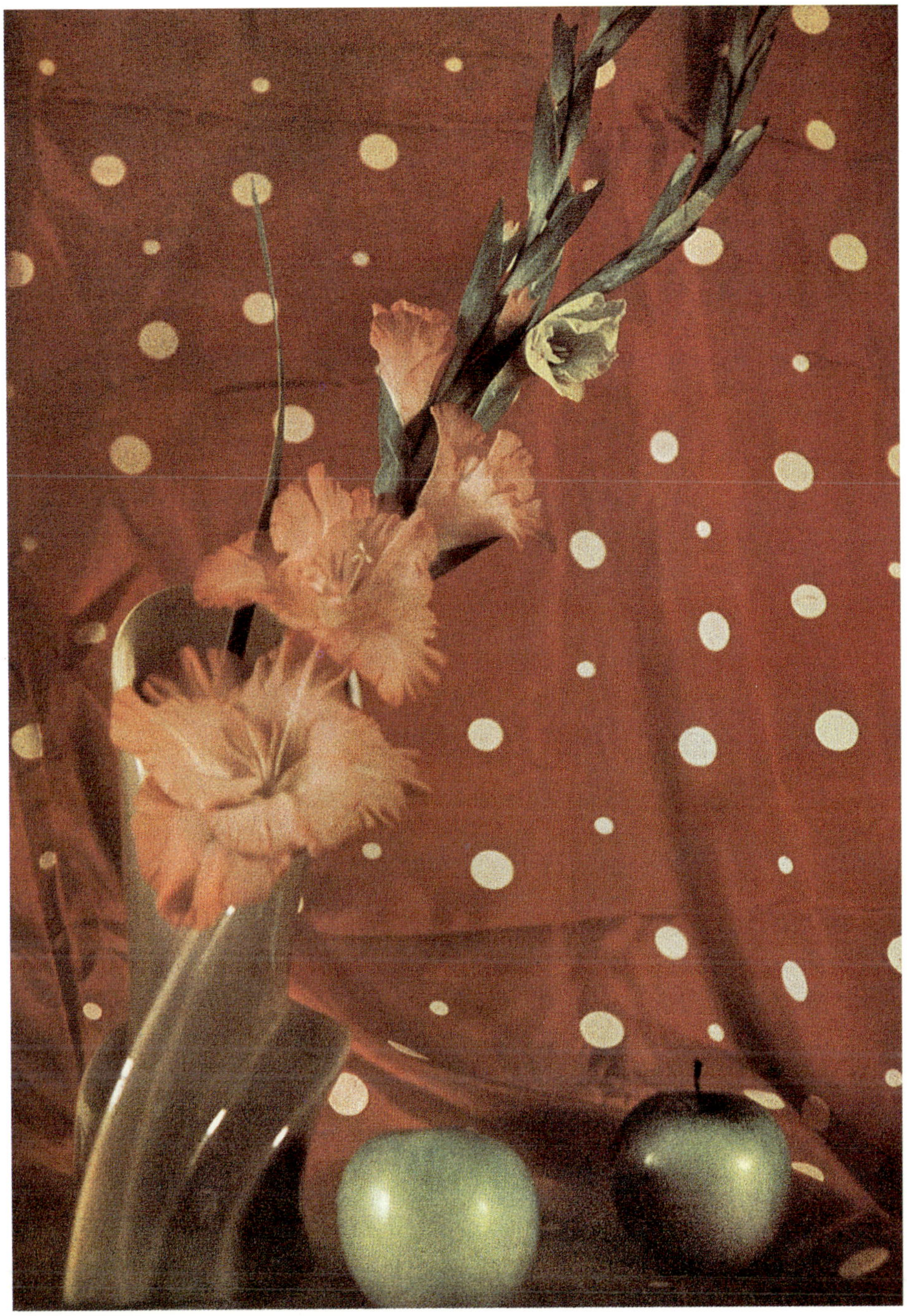

ROSEMARY, BRACELETS 1984

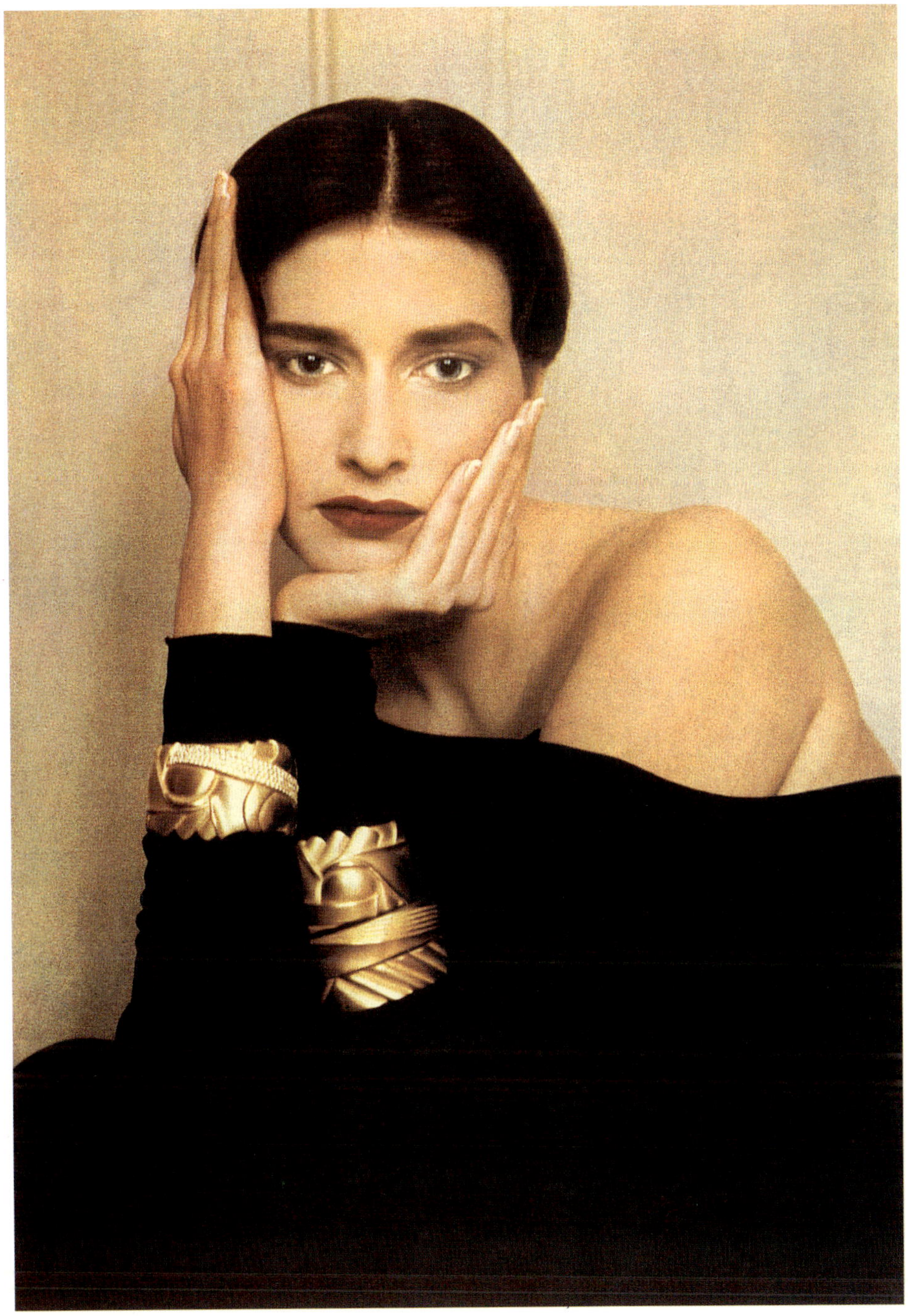

ODALISQUE 1986

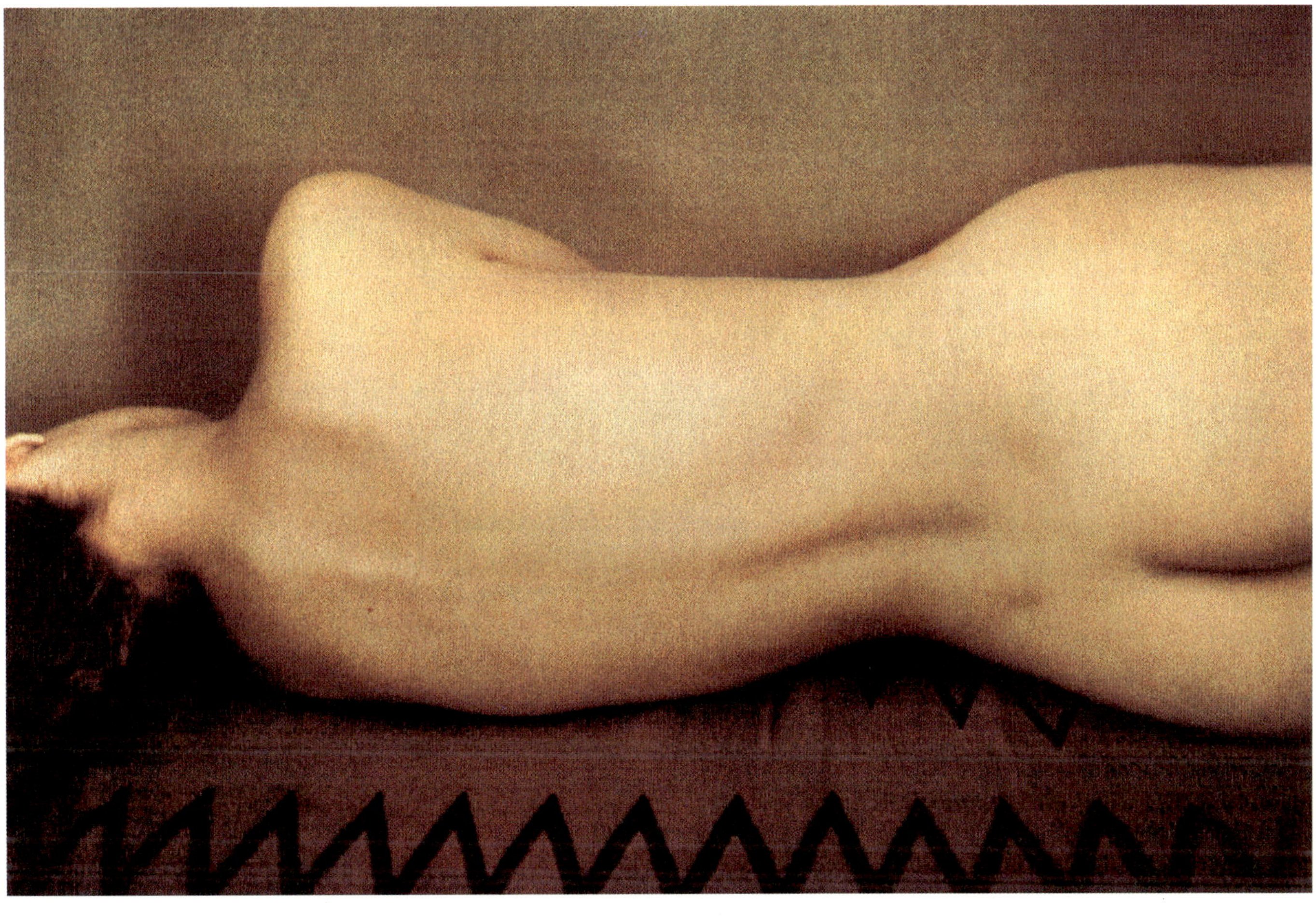

STELLA, HALLOWEEN ANGEL 1984

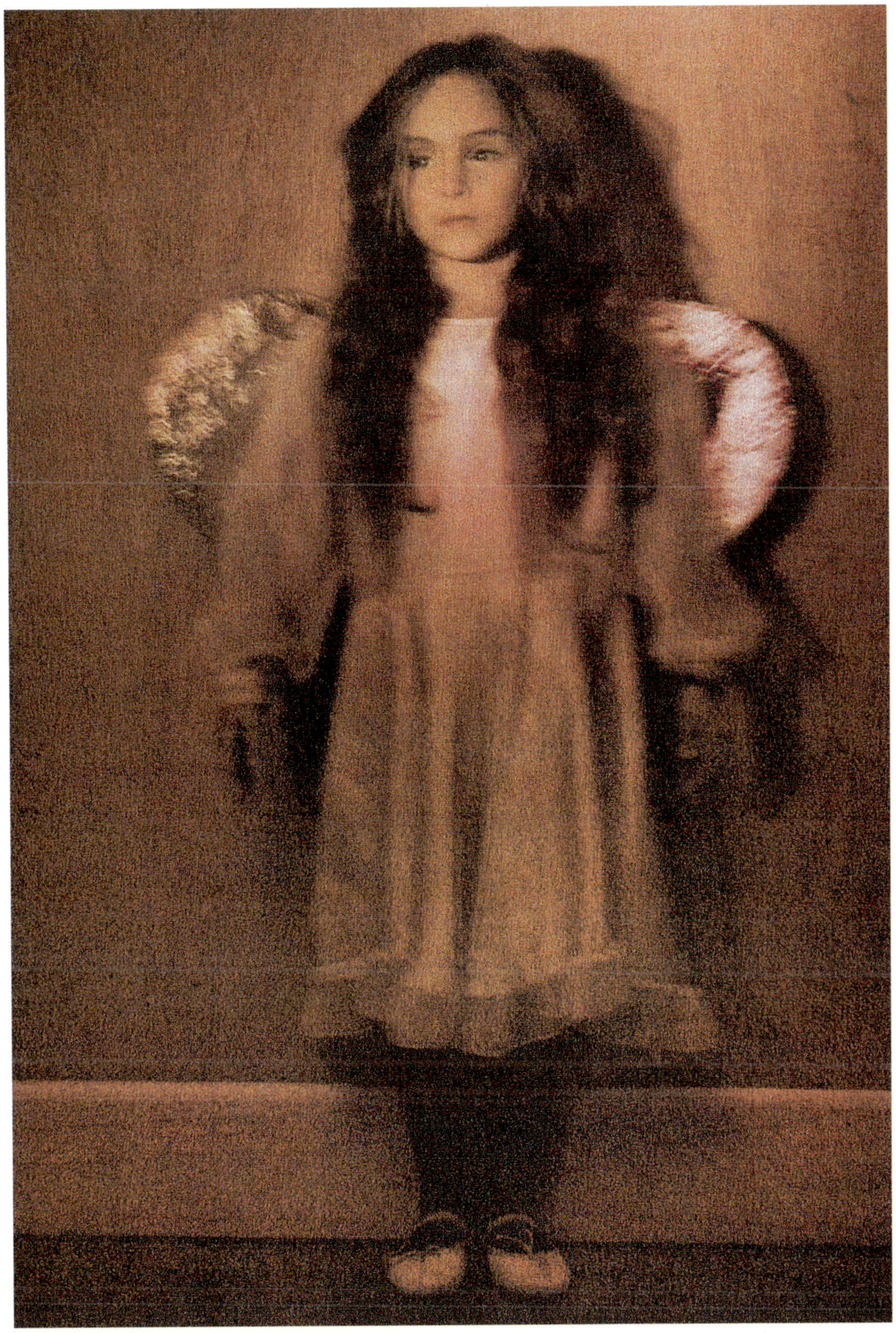

KATHLEEN CARR 1985

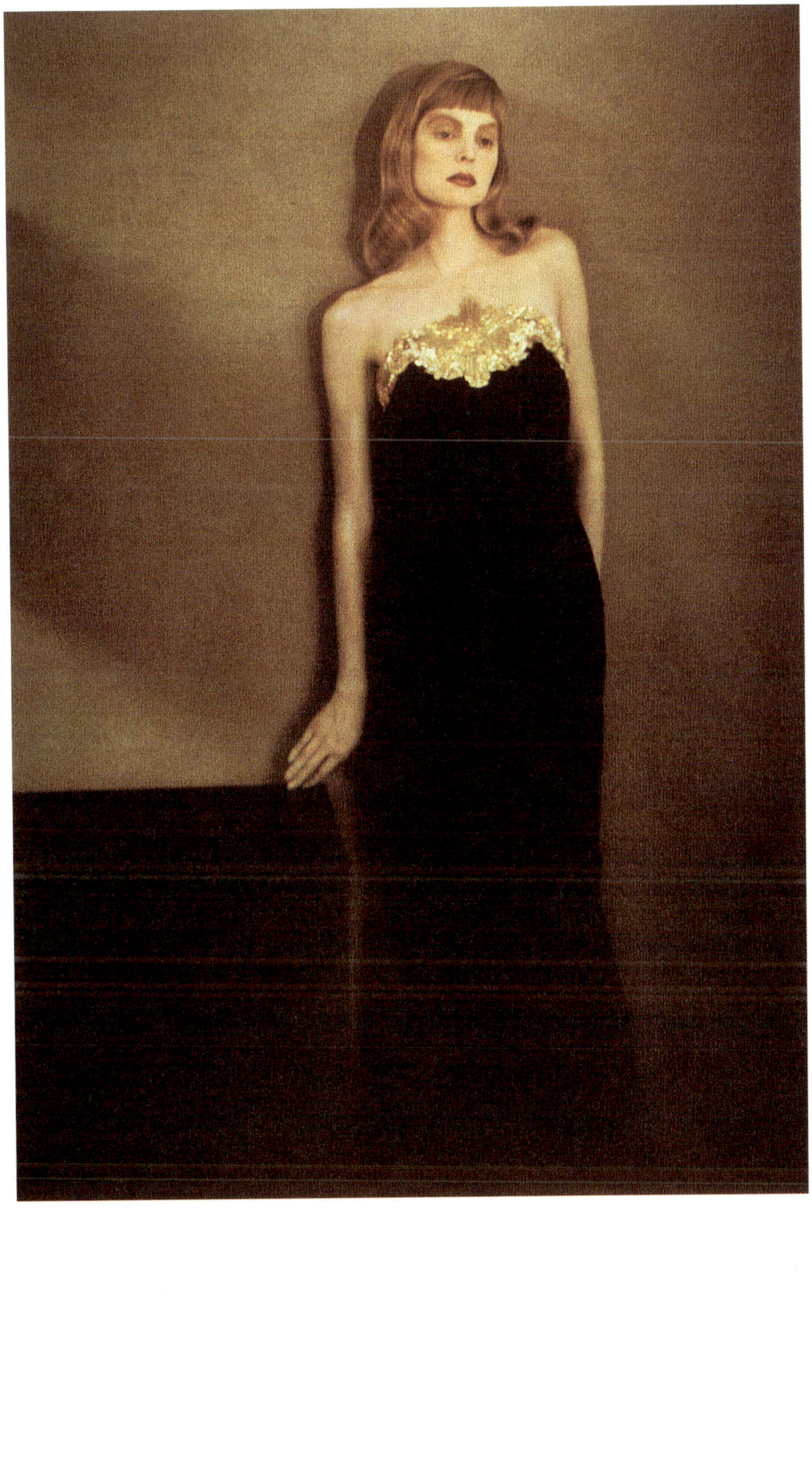

JOKO, PASSION 1985

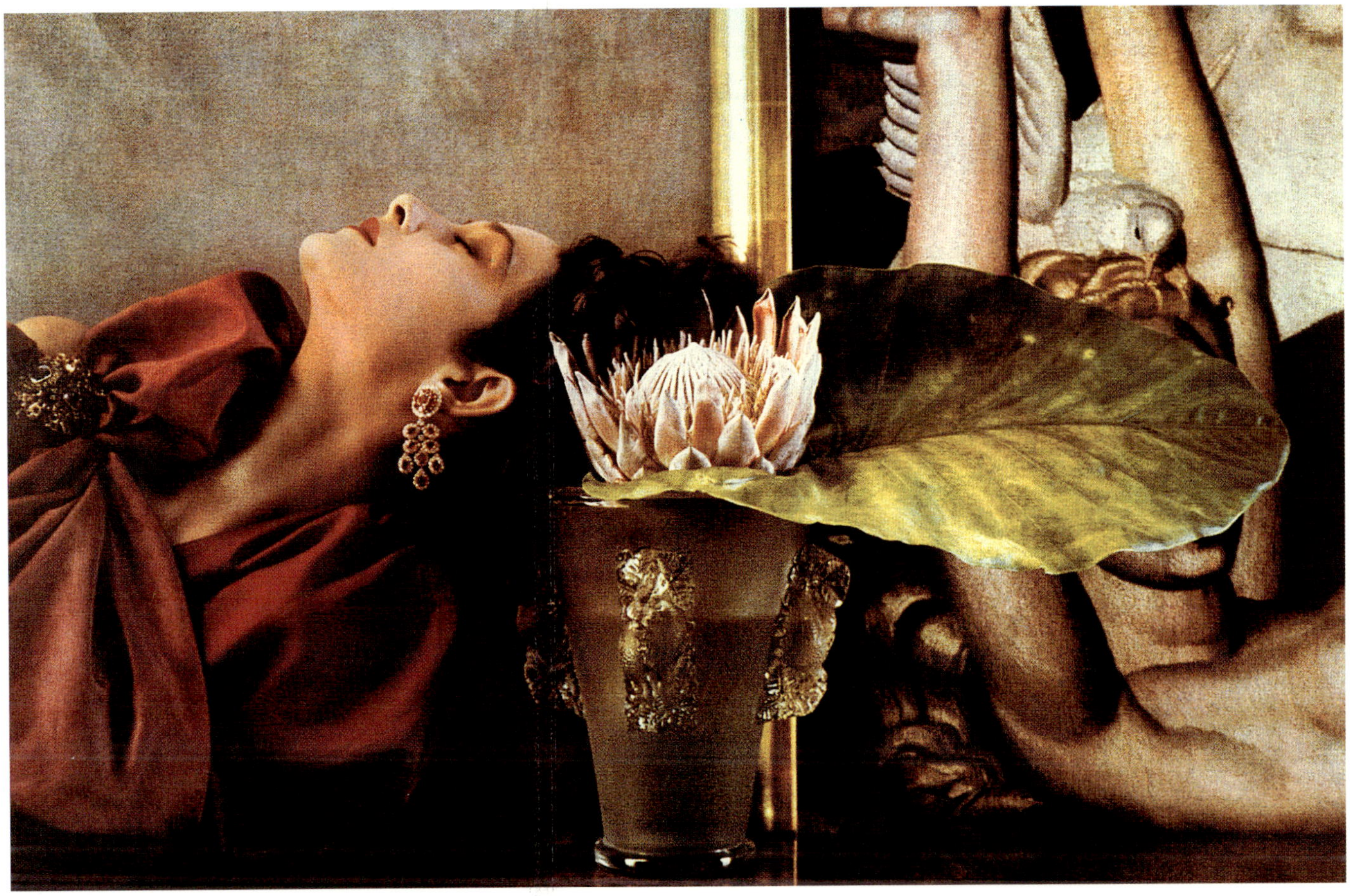

MONDRIAN ORCHID 1982

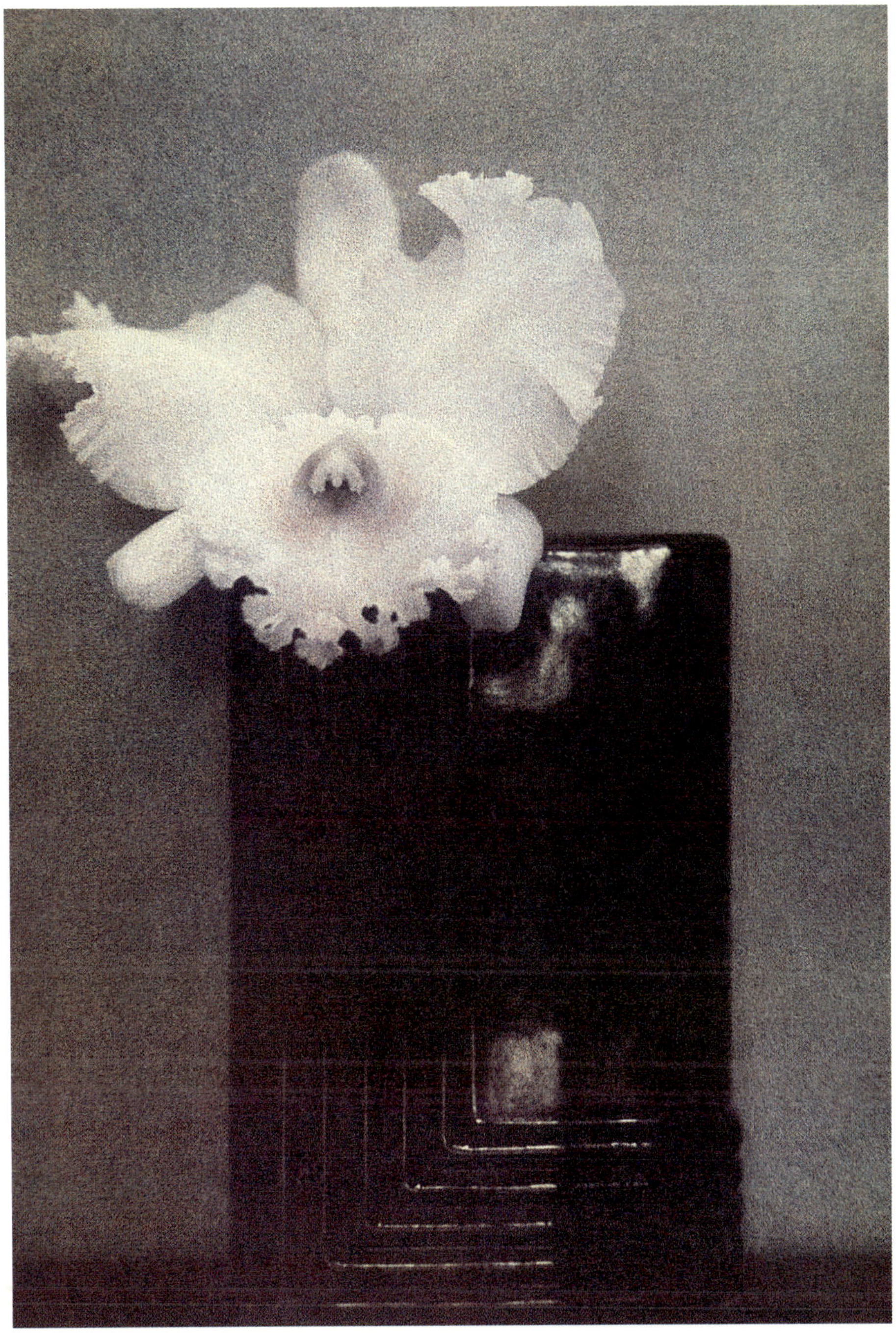

RAVEN ASLEEP 1984

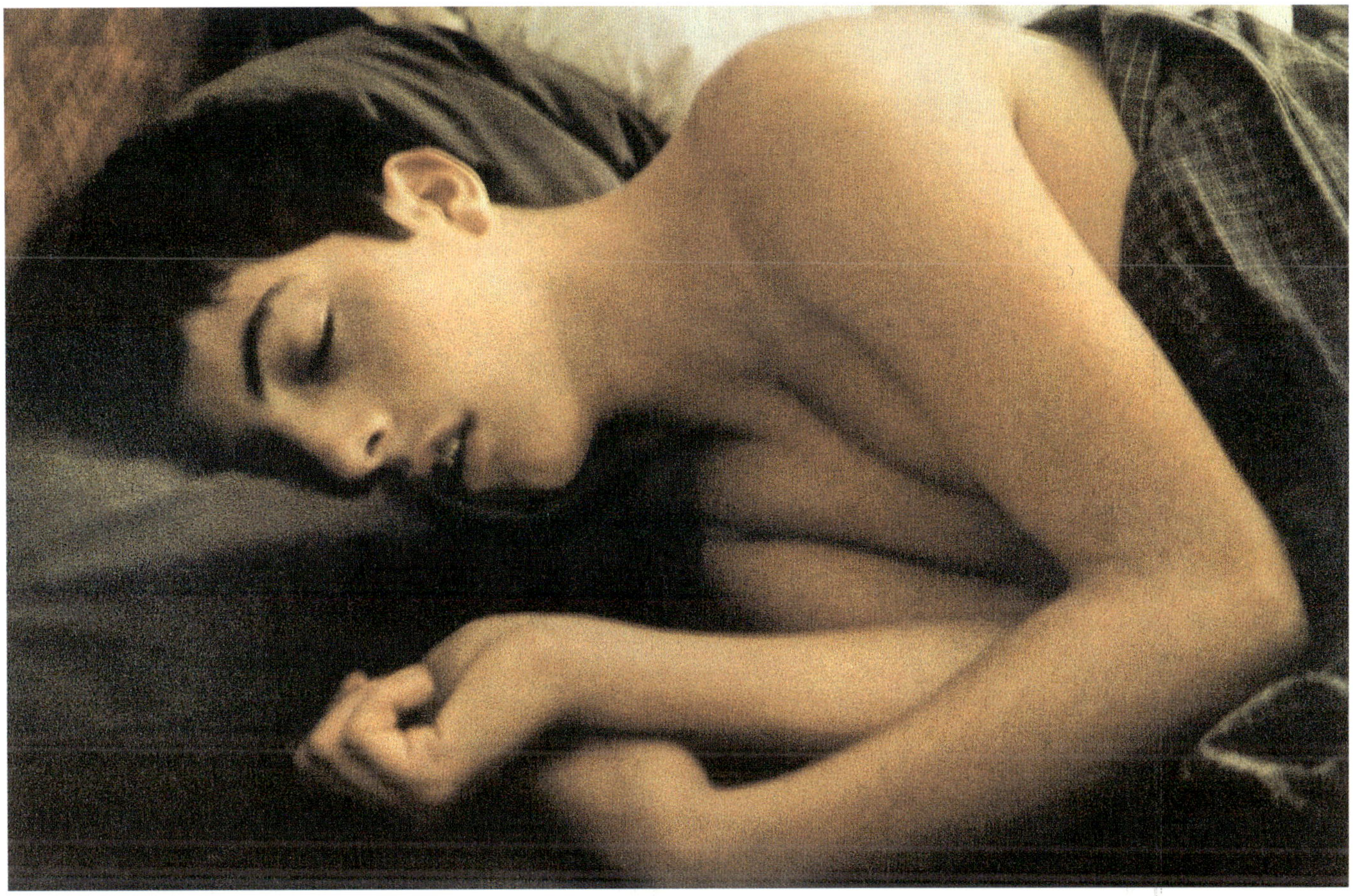

ART DECO LADY 1984

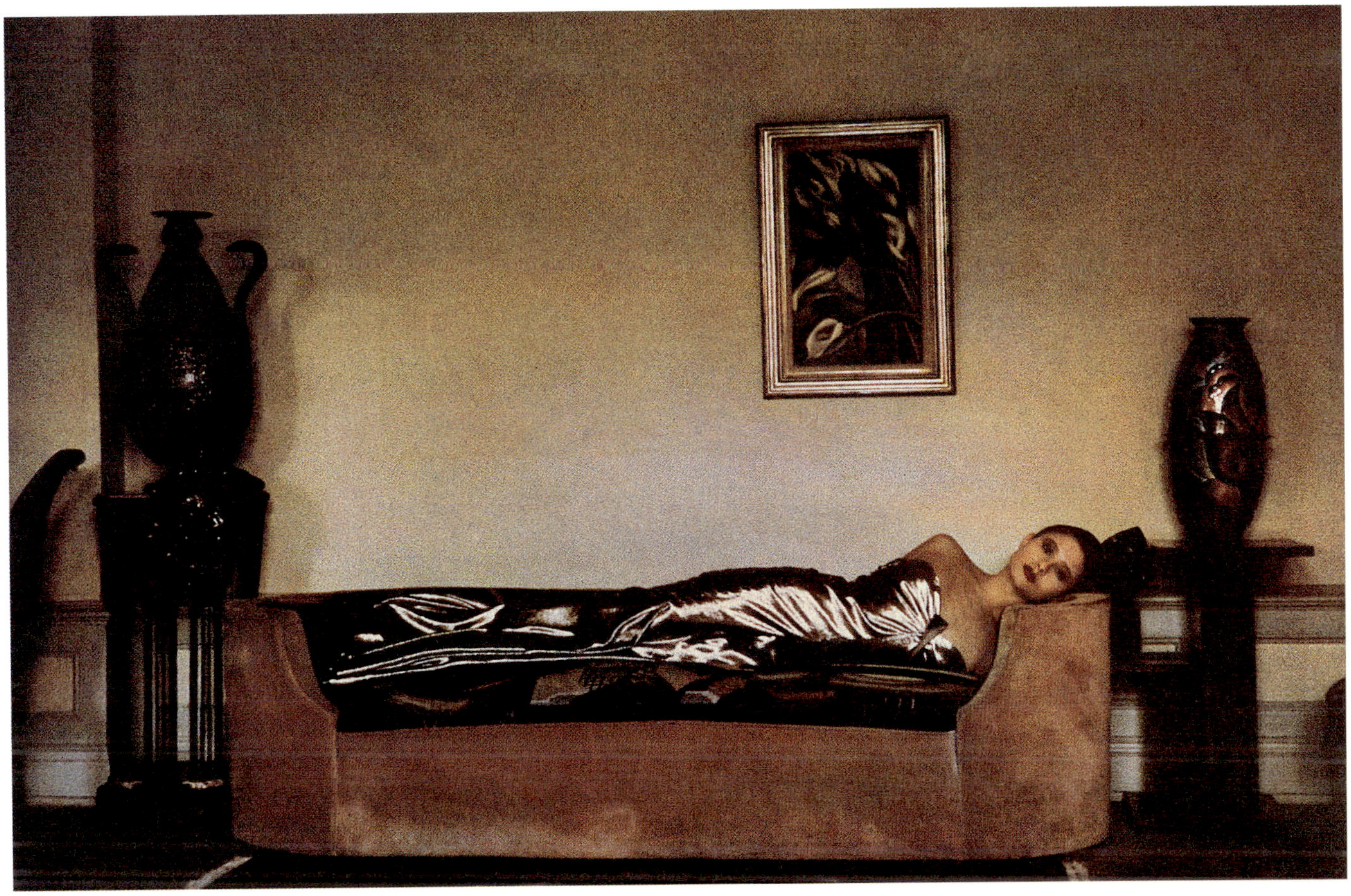

DUNAND STILL LIFE 1985

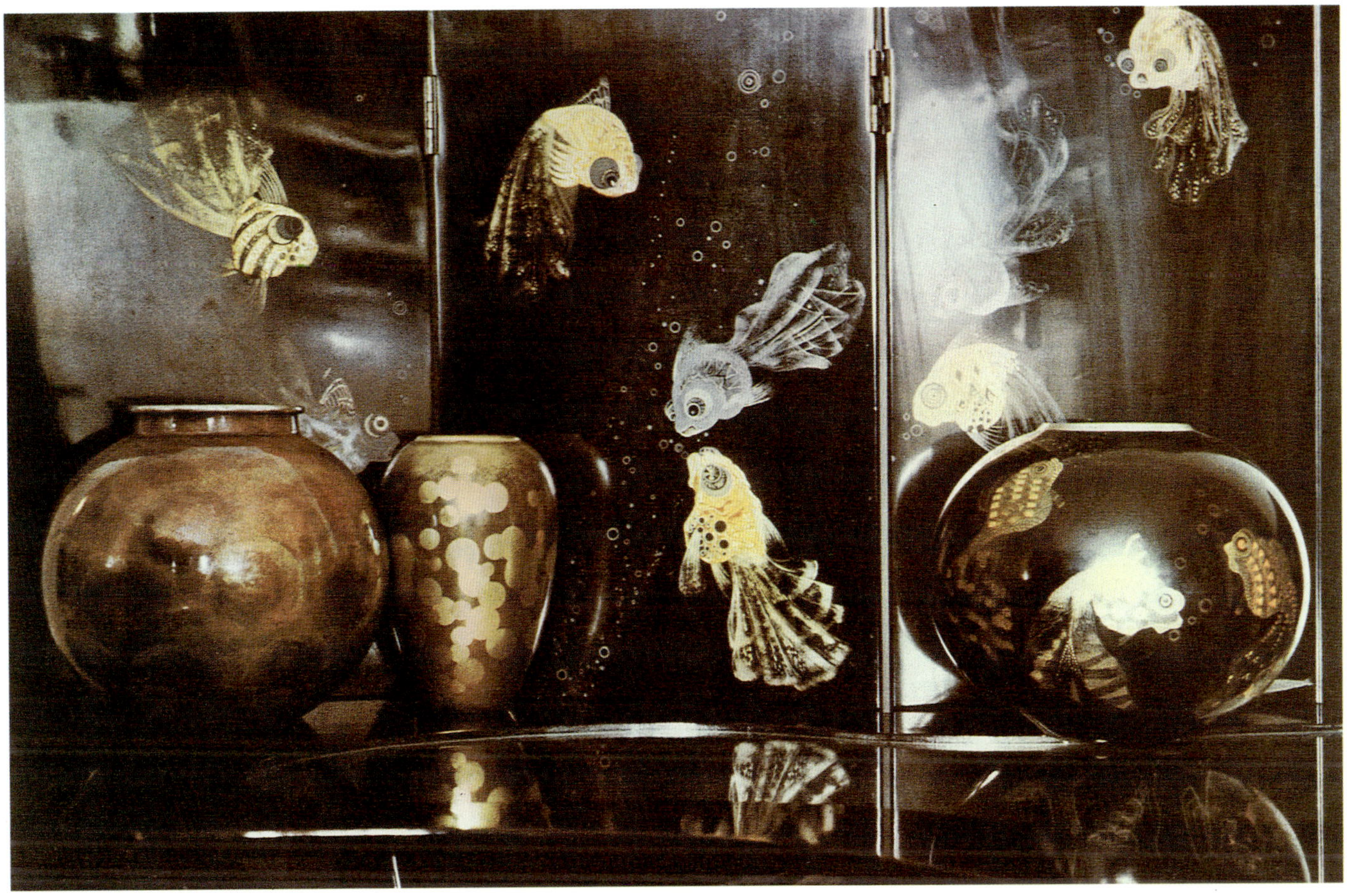

SAXAPHONE VASE 1985

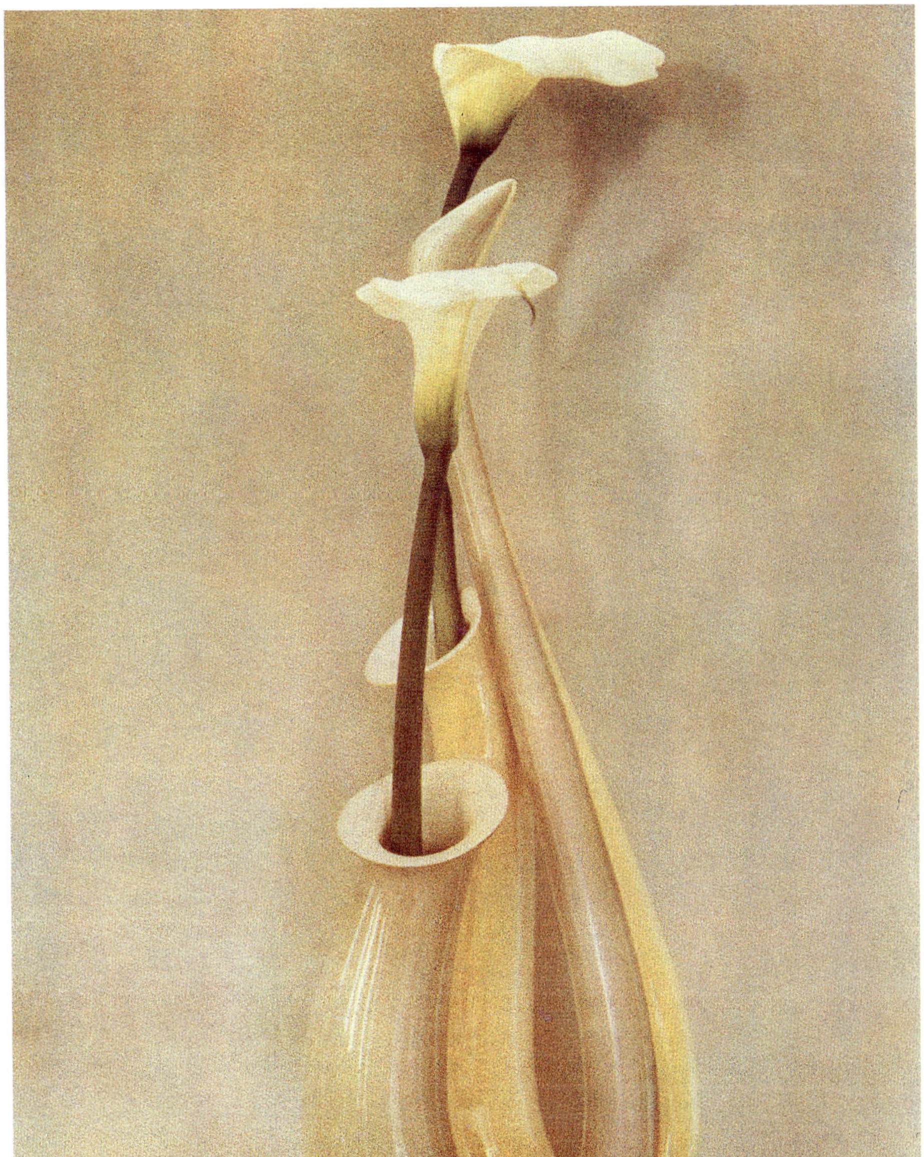

UMA, PATOU DRESS 1986

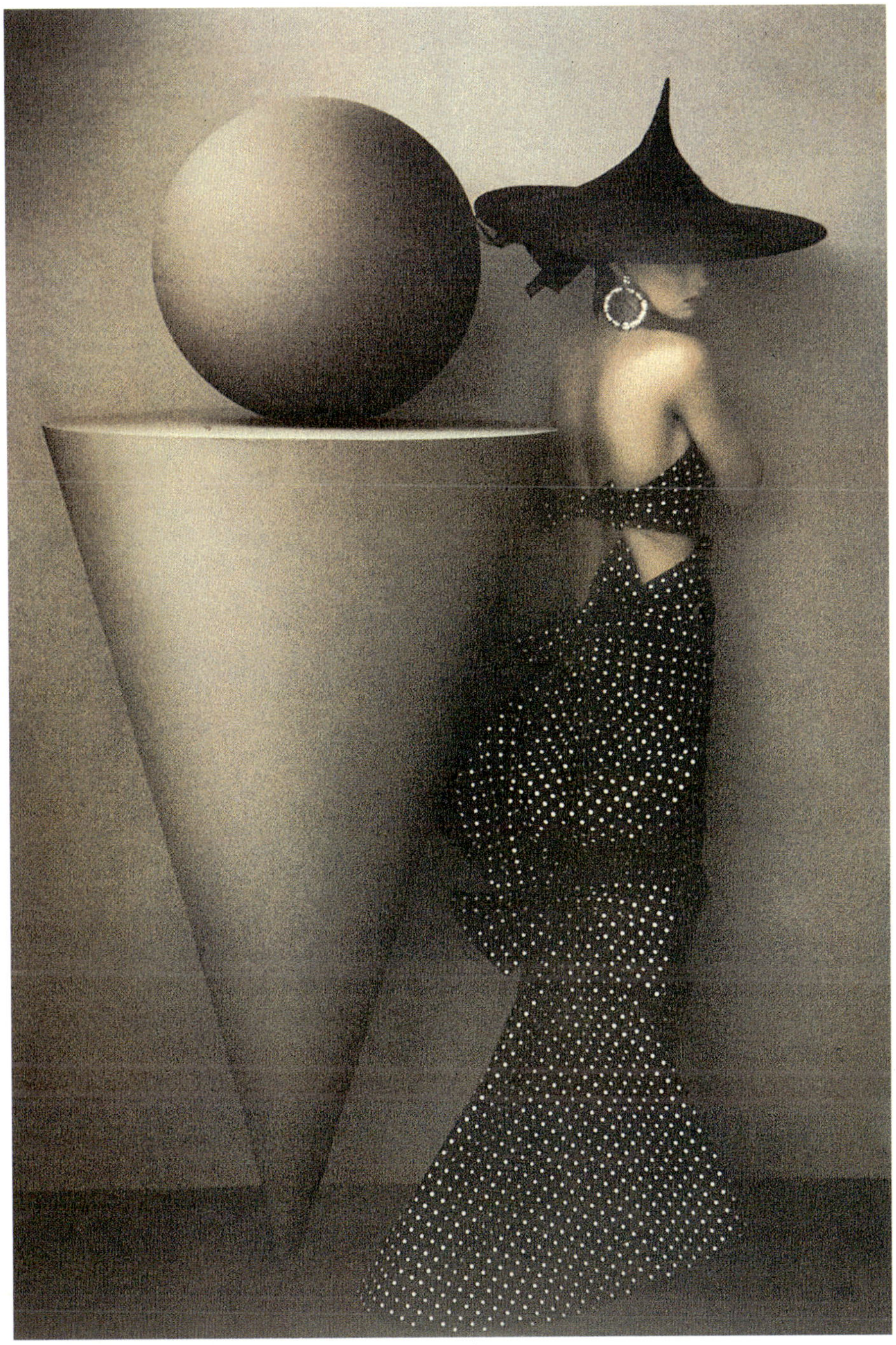

MOUILLE, PROTOTYPES 1985

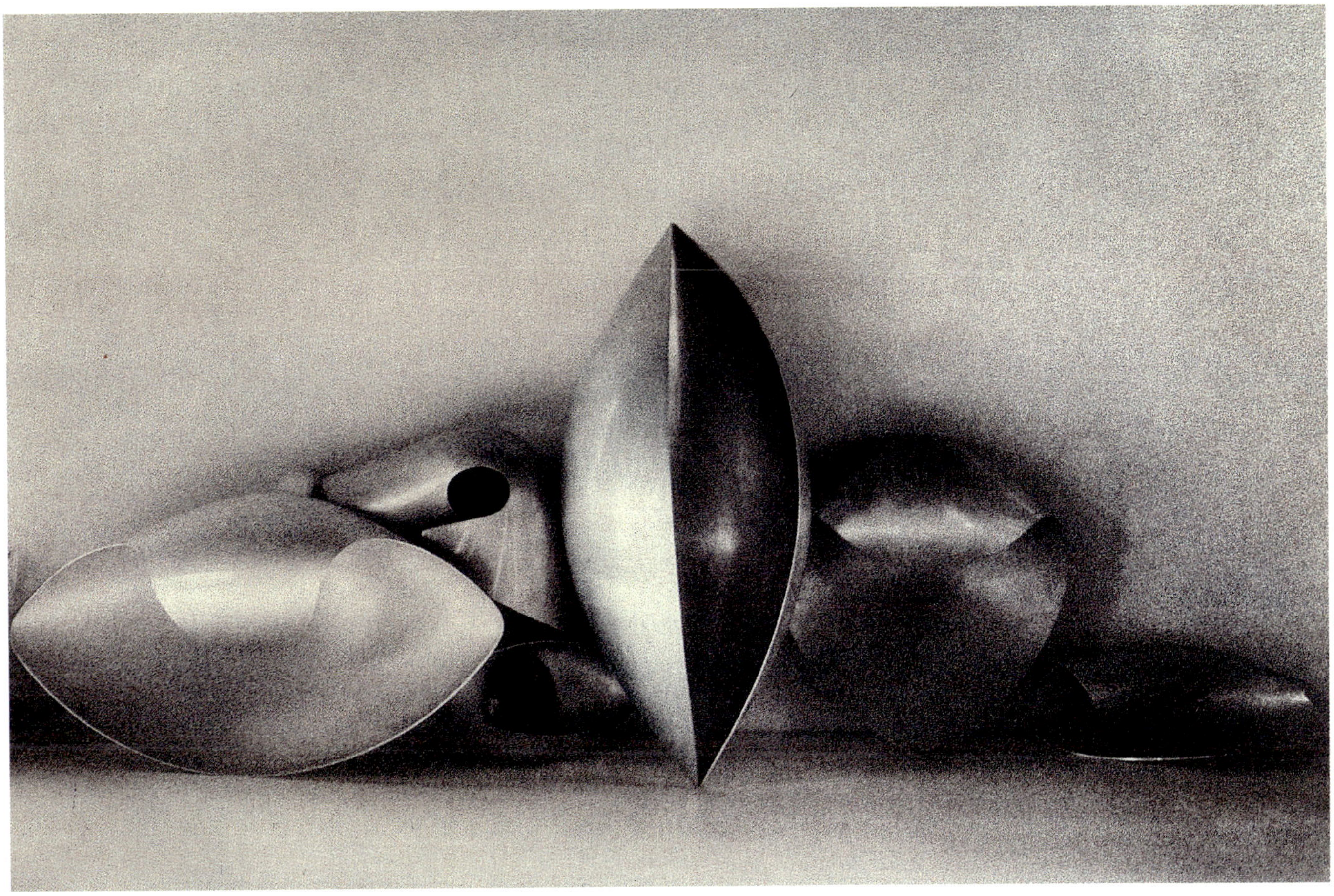

TIME 1988

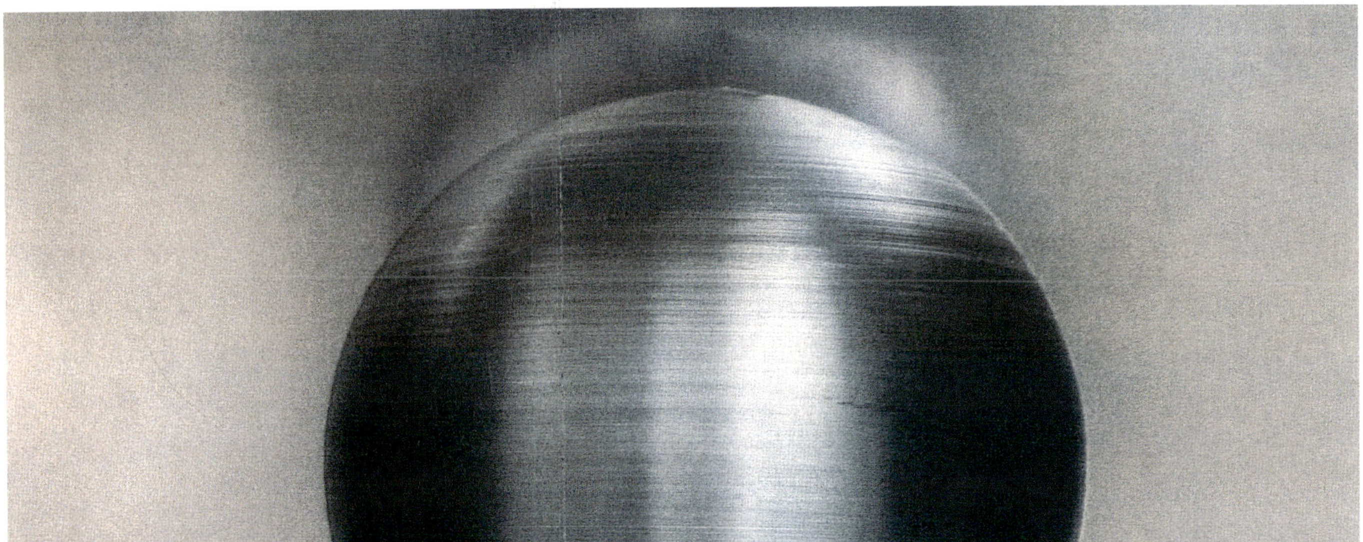

FASHION 1988

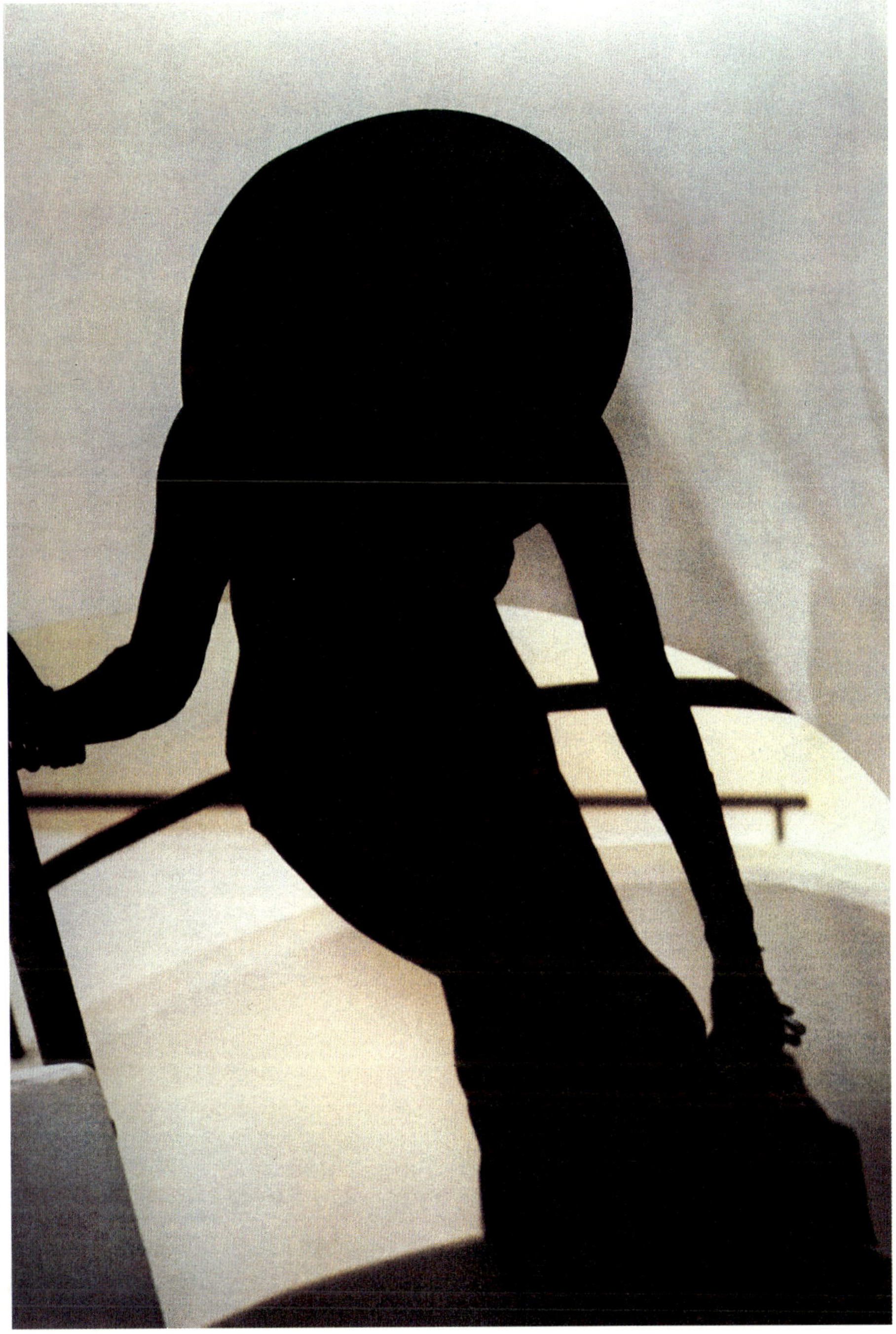

NUDE, HESTER 1987

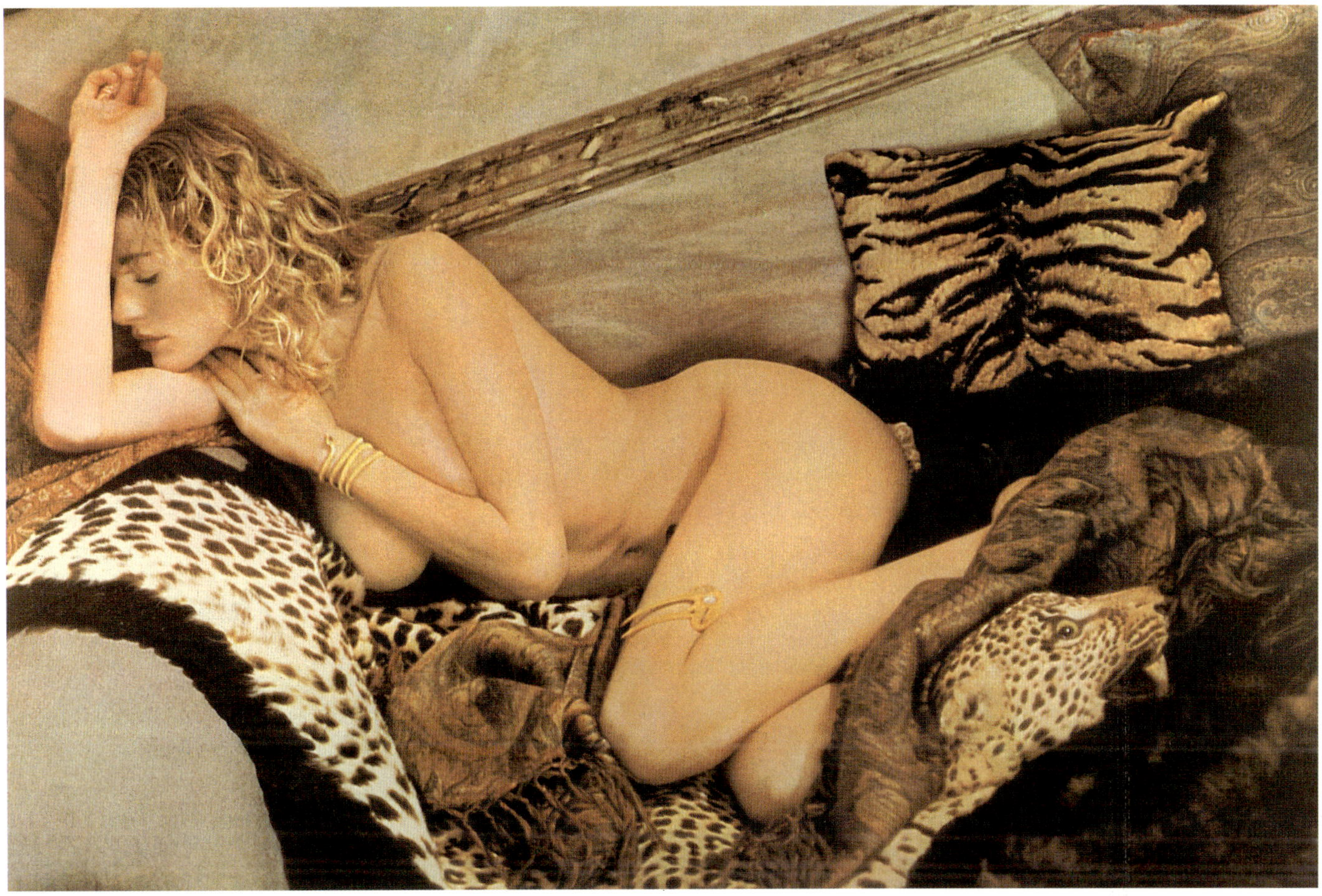

STELLA, MOUILLE SHAPE 1986

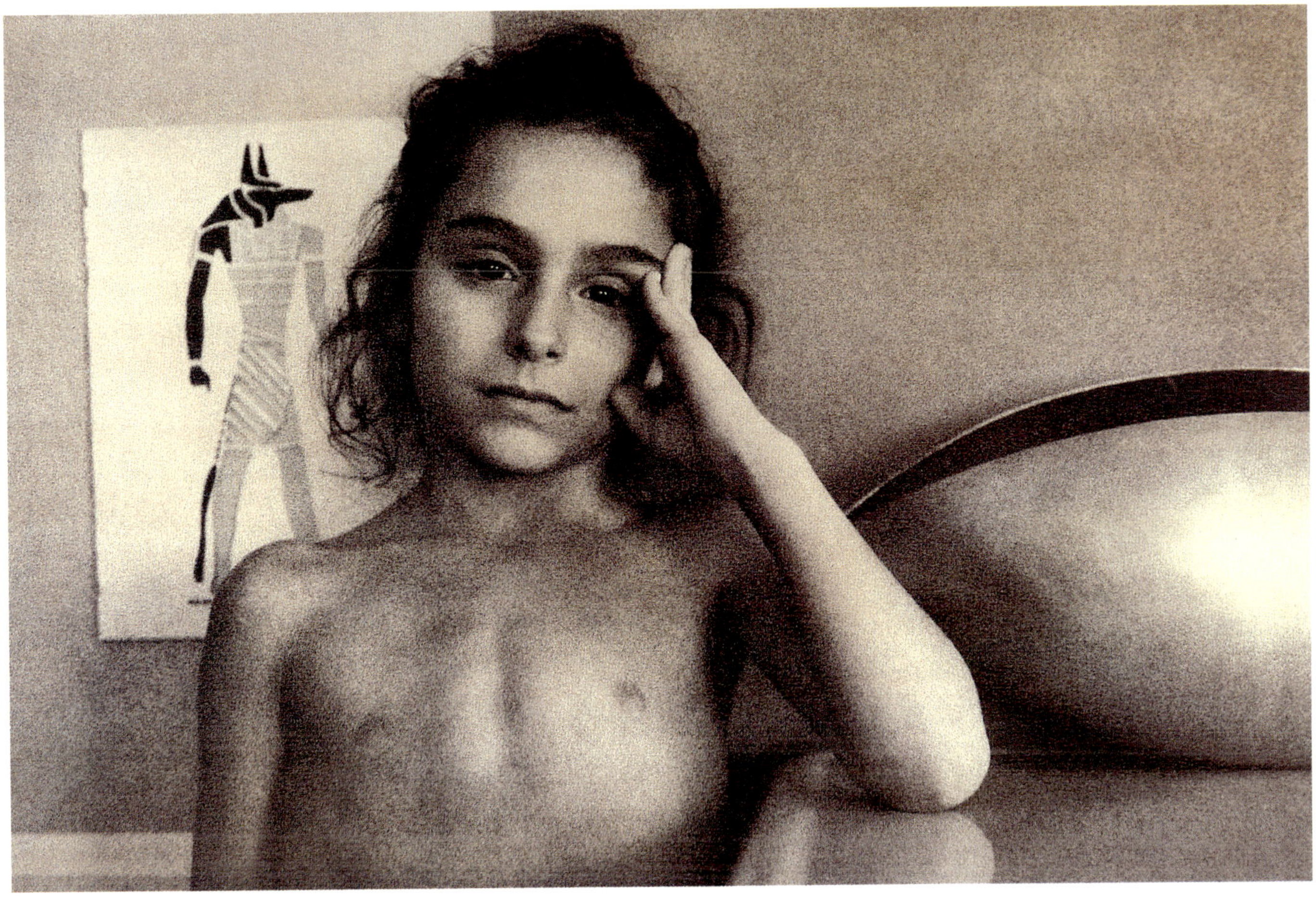

TRIXIE, STEEL BALL 1988

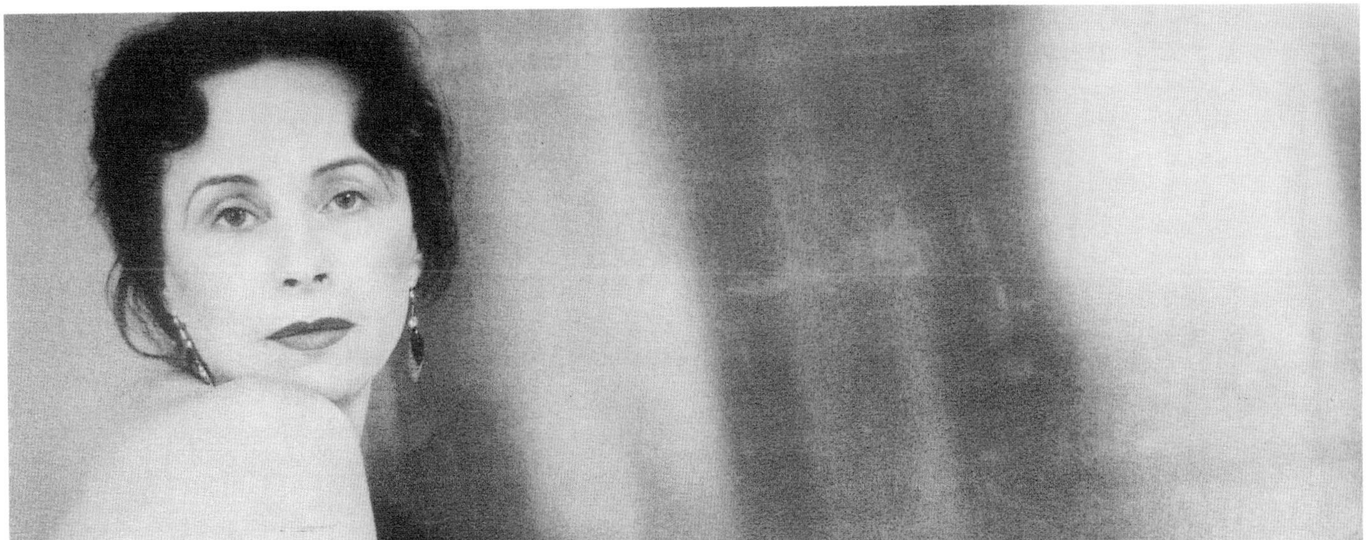

RICK, DYNAMO SERIES 1989

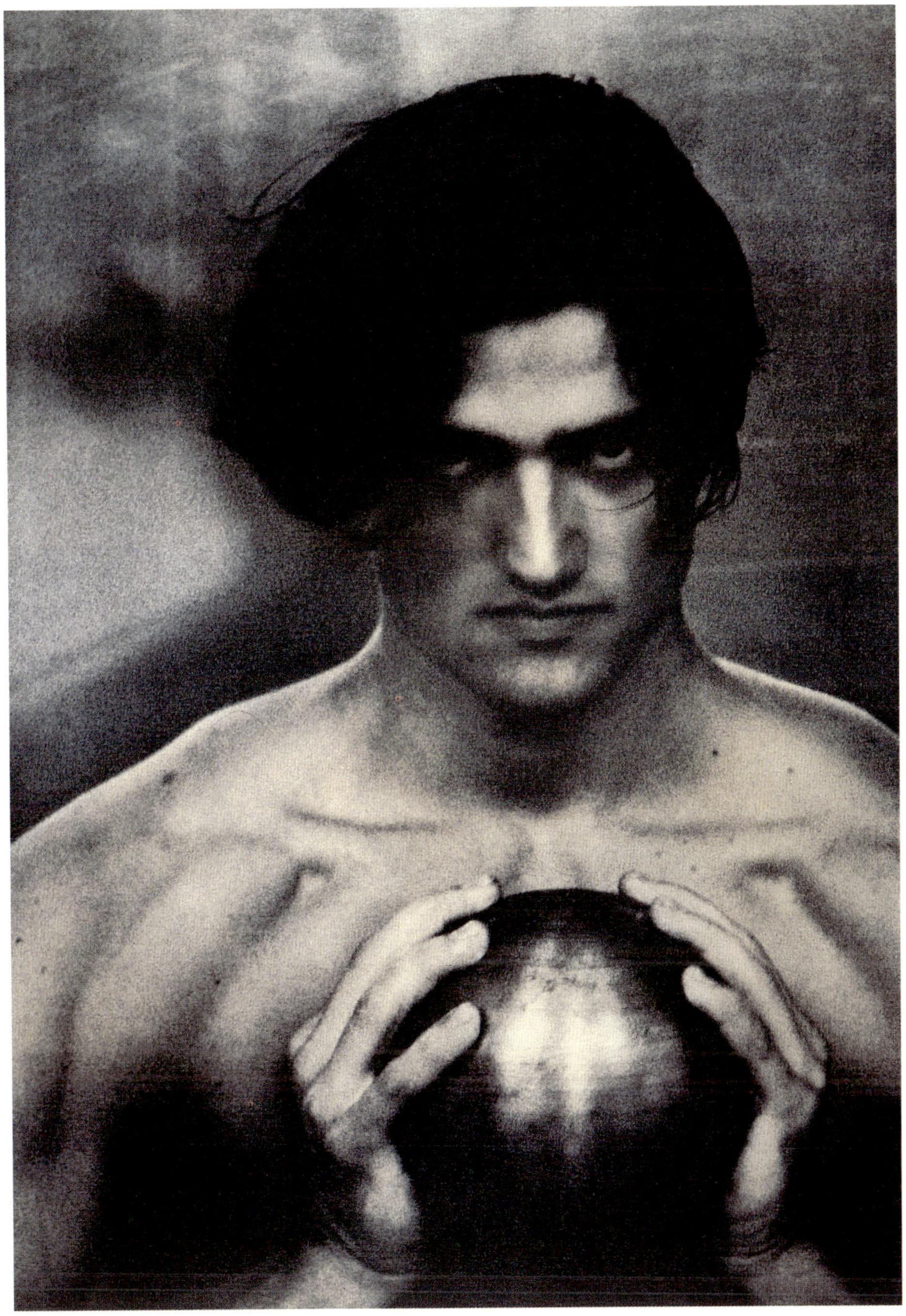

FENDI HUOMO 1988

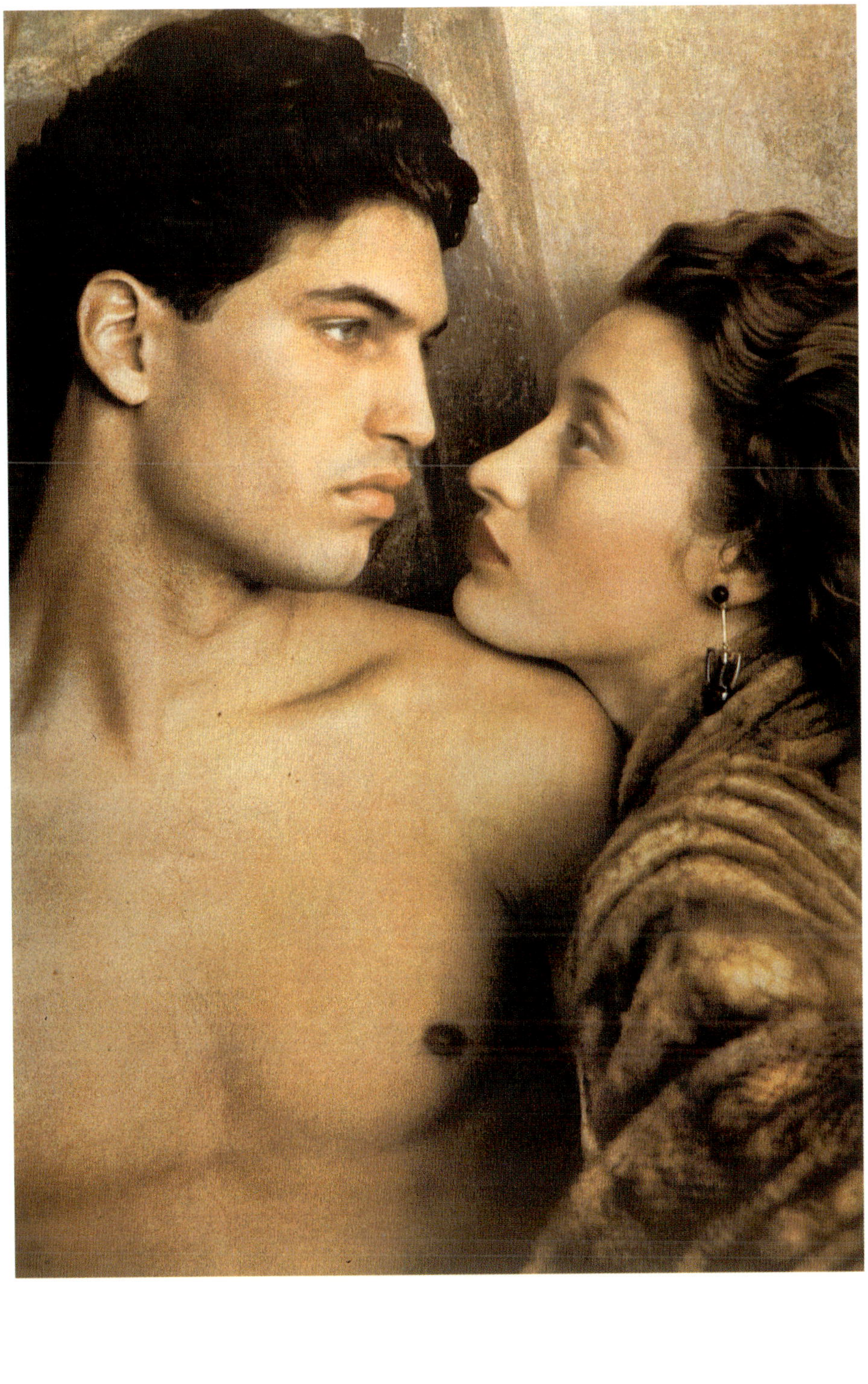

JOSIE 1989

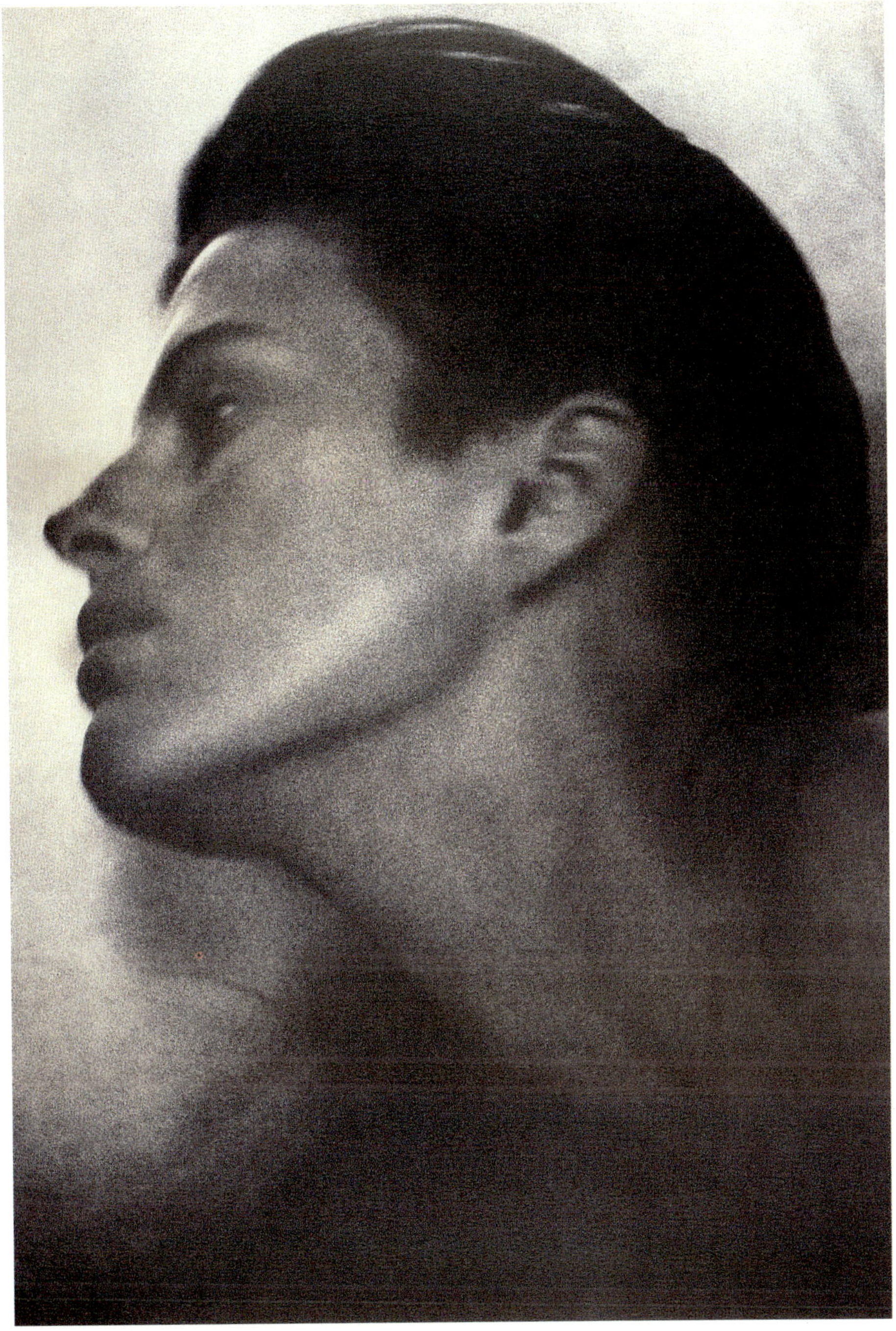

THE PASSION OF ROME 1986

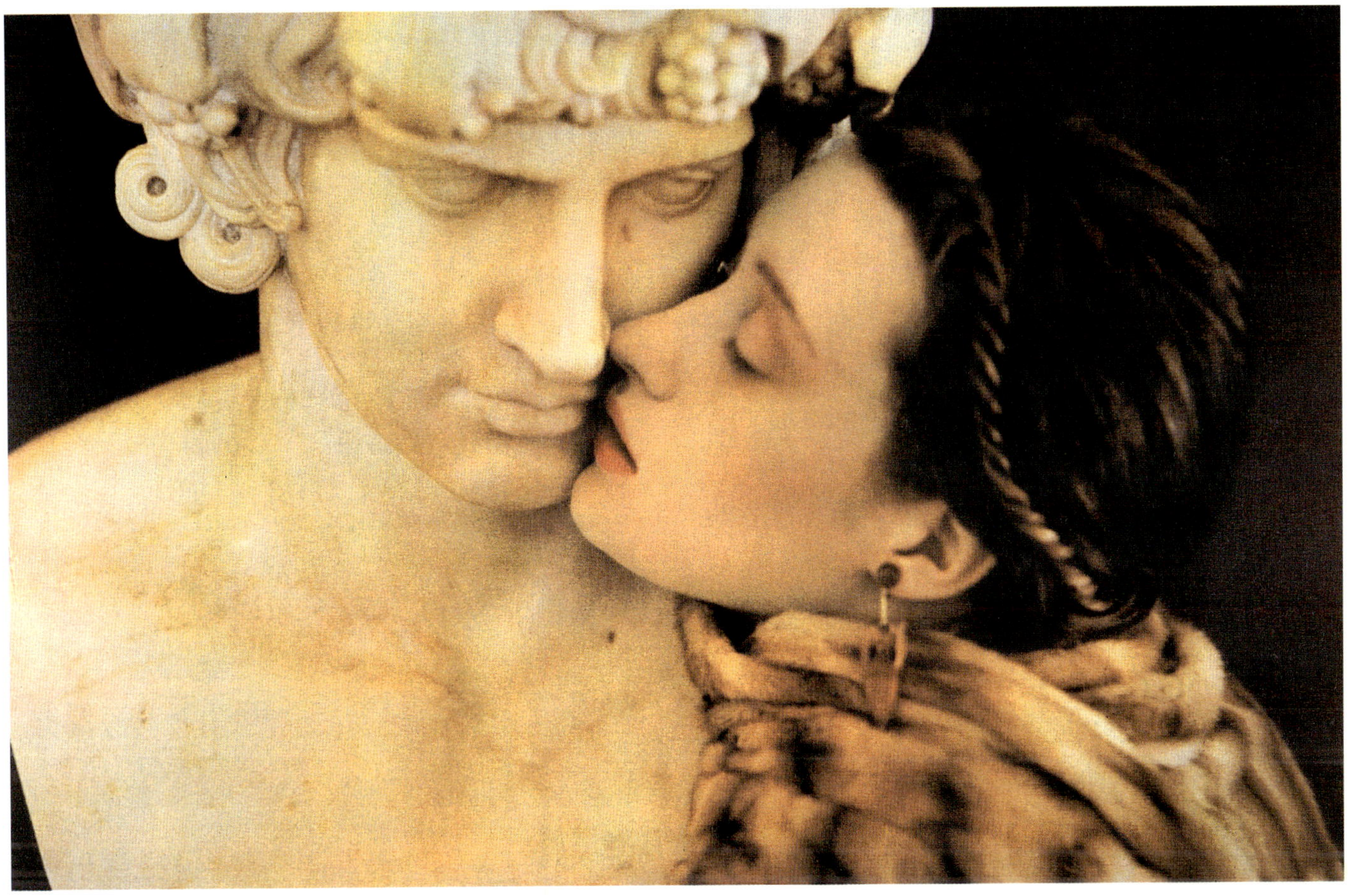

ANA, TORSO 1989

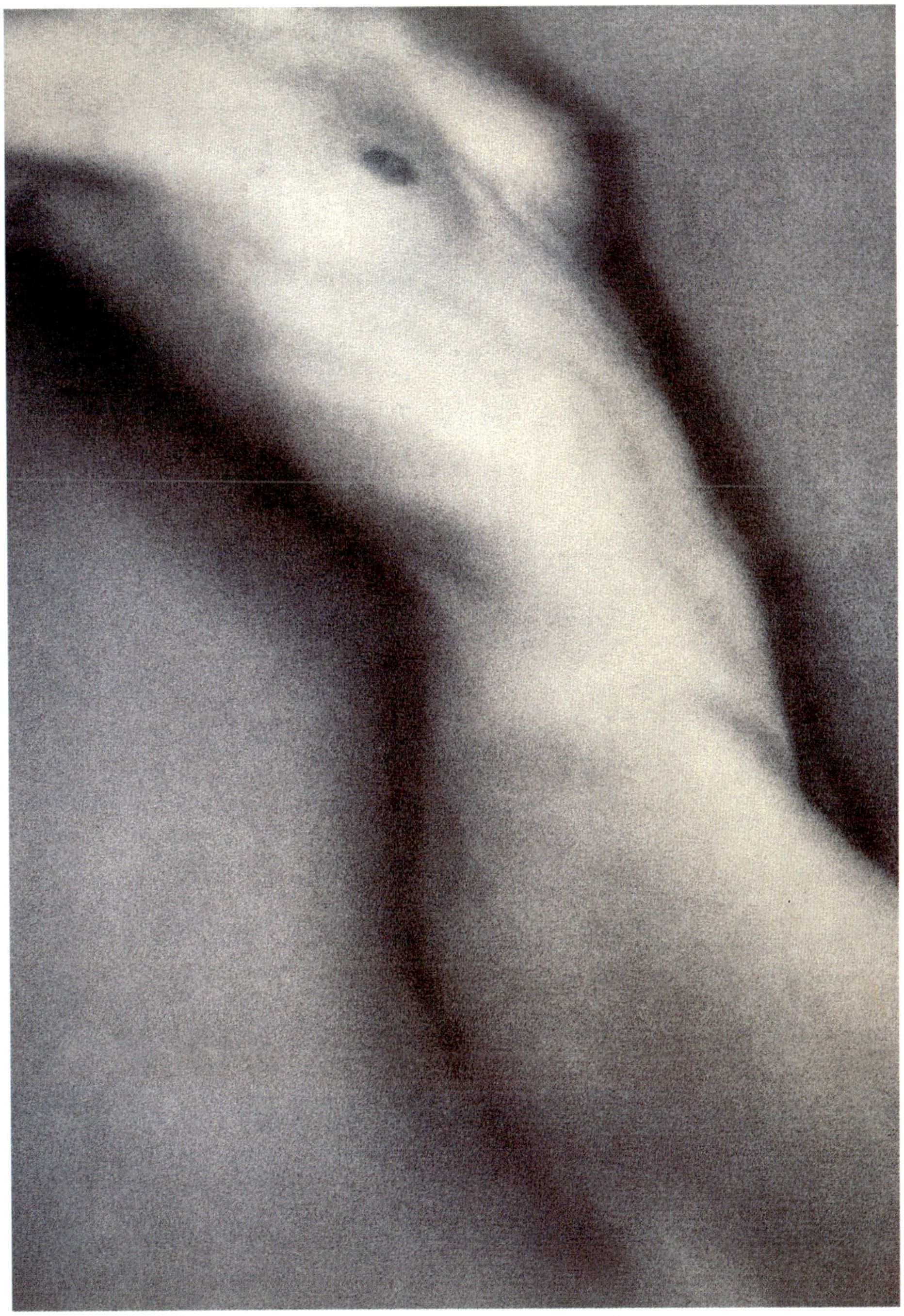

MARIE SOPHIE 1986

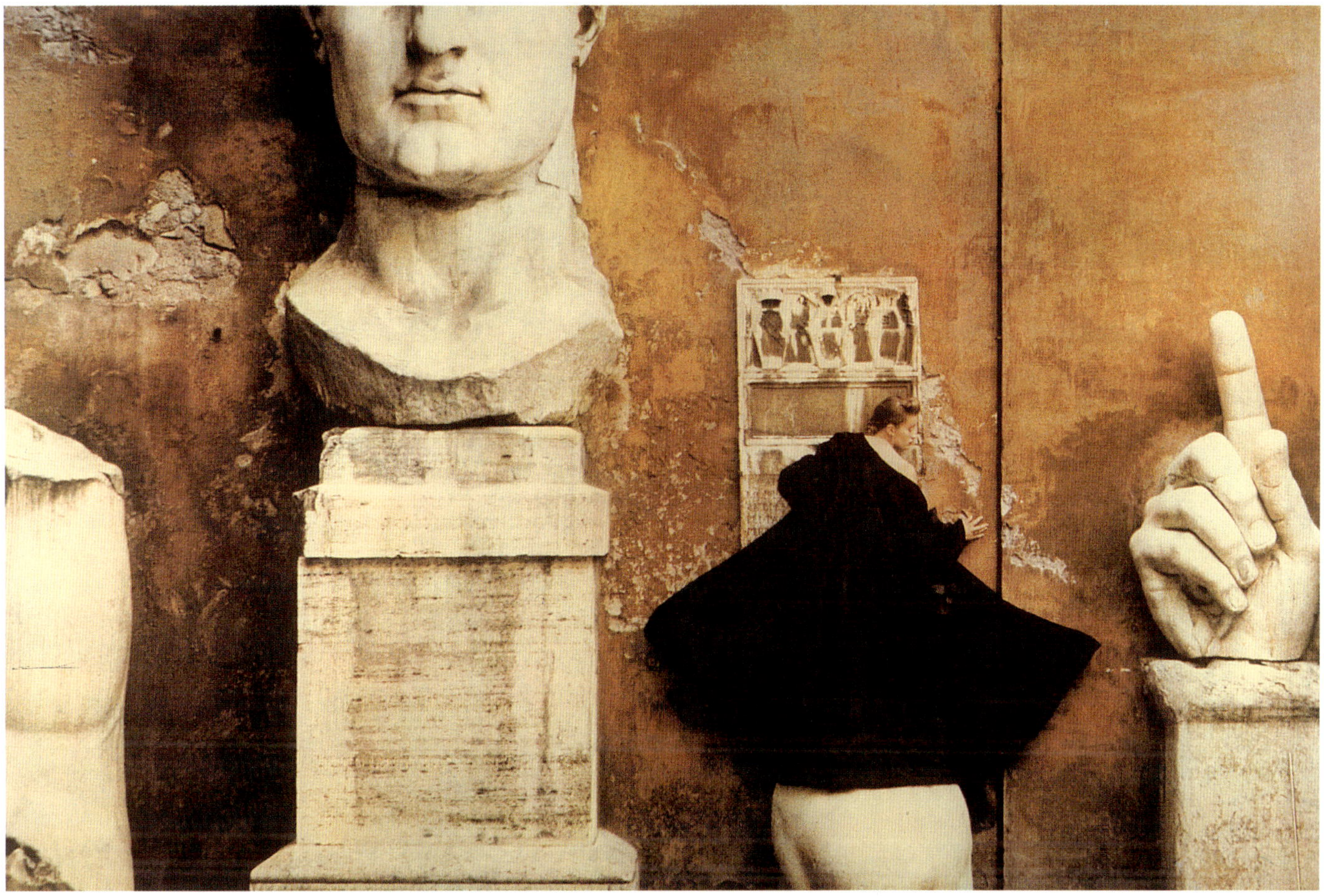

MARIE SOPHIE 1986

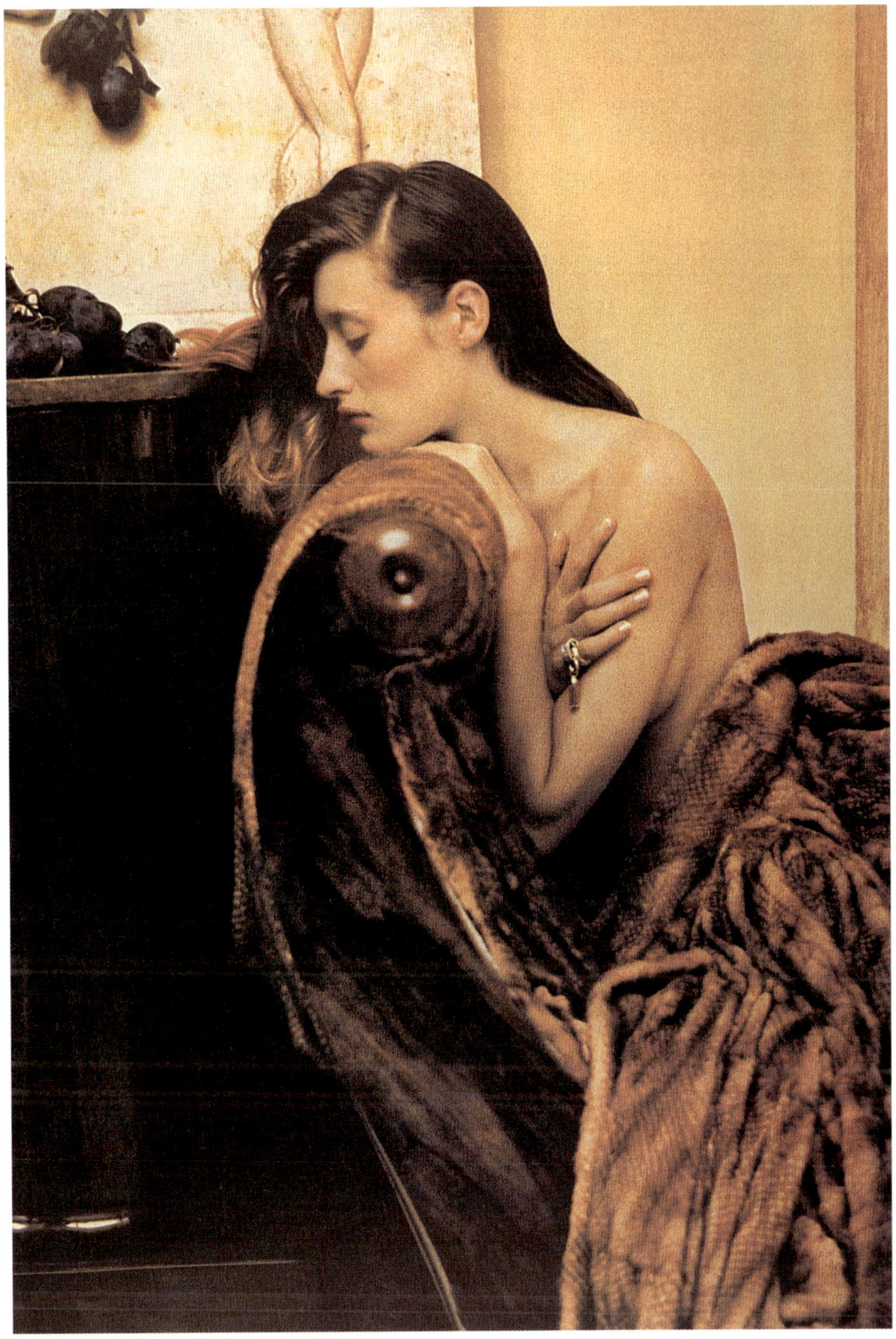

MARIE SOPHIE 1986

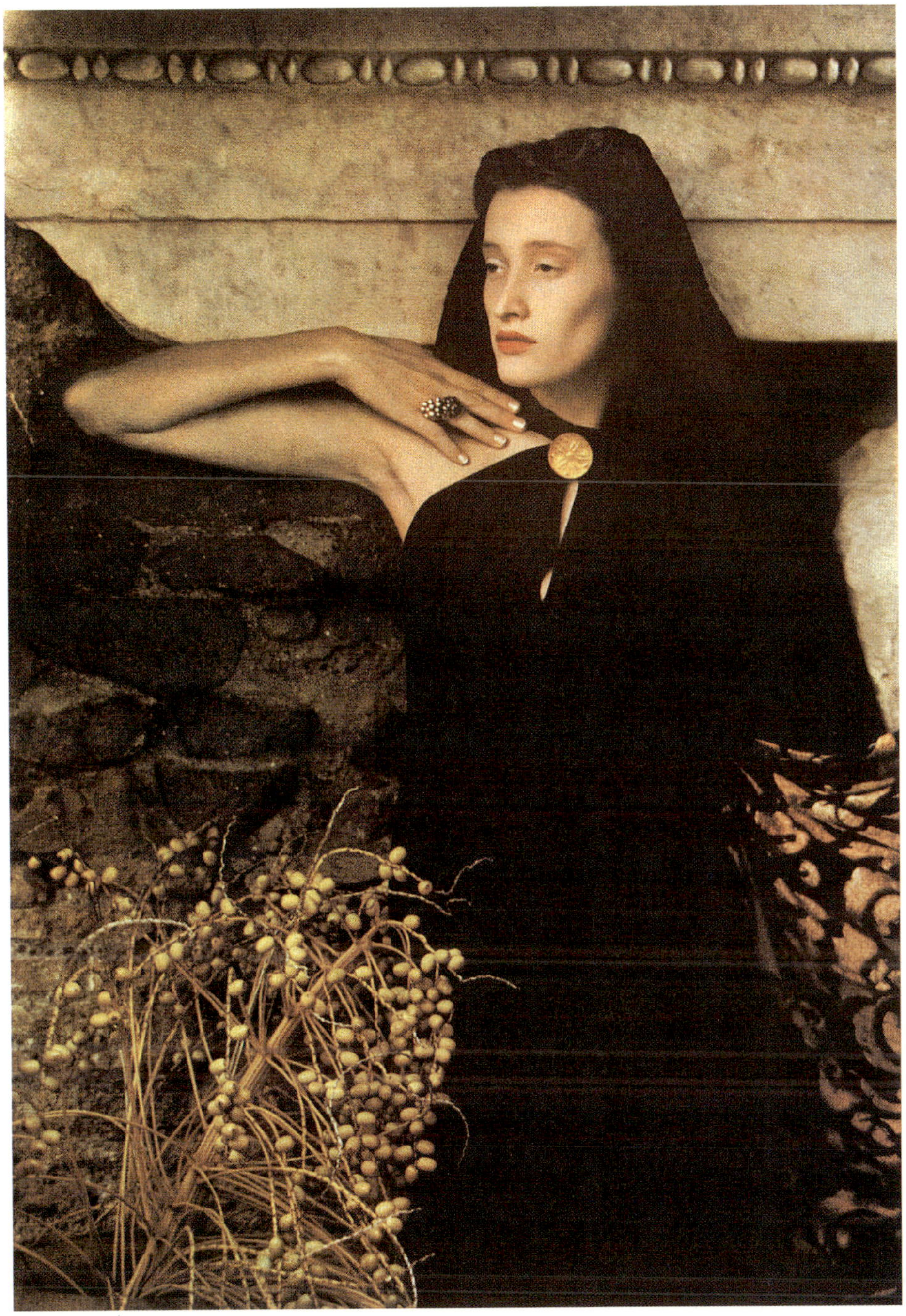

ELAINE, LEE MILLER 1988

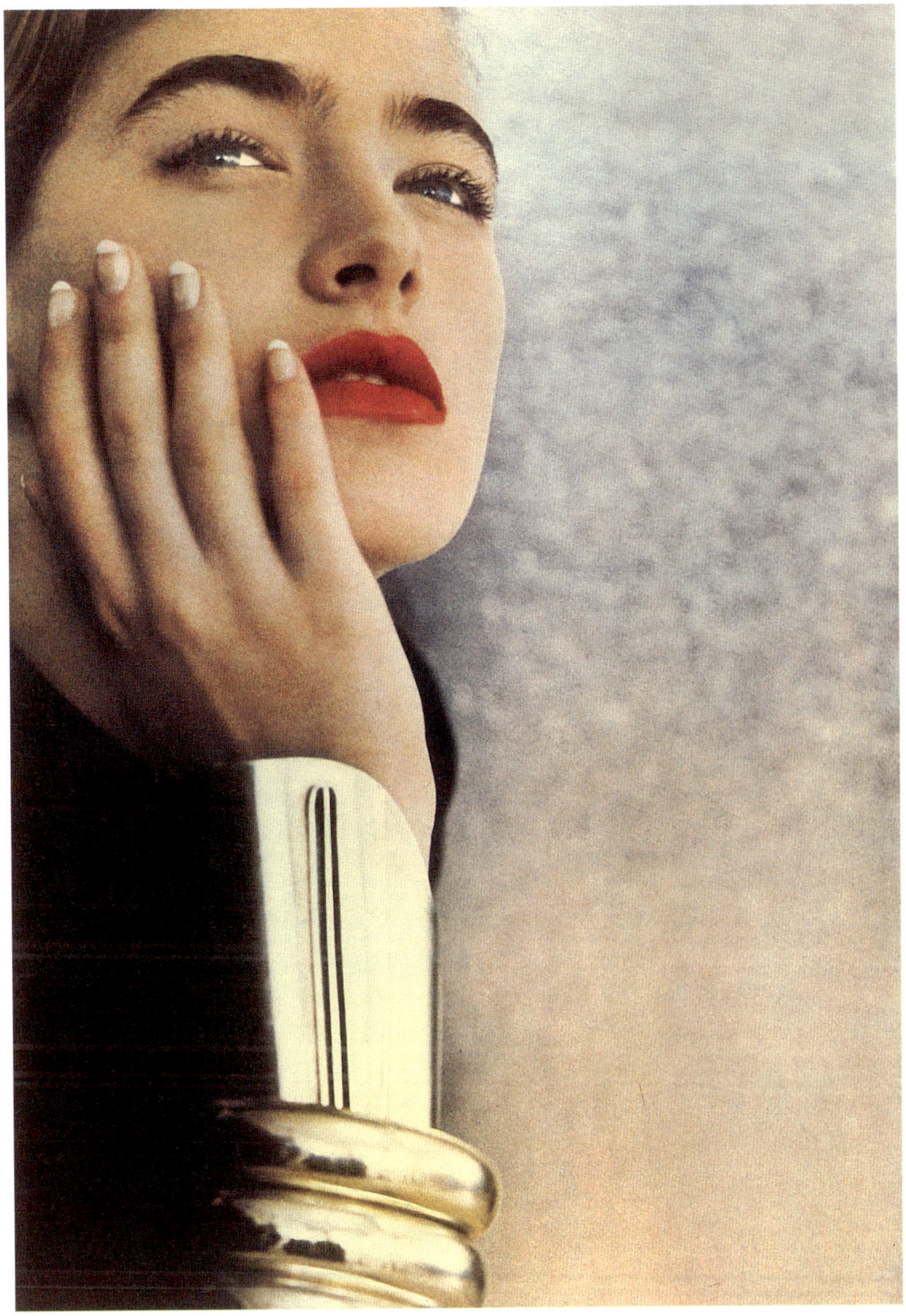

STELLA, LITTLE BEACH 1989

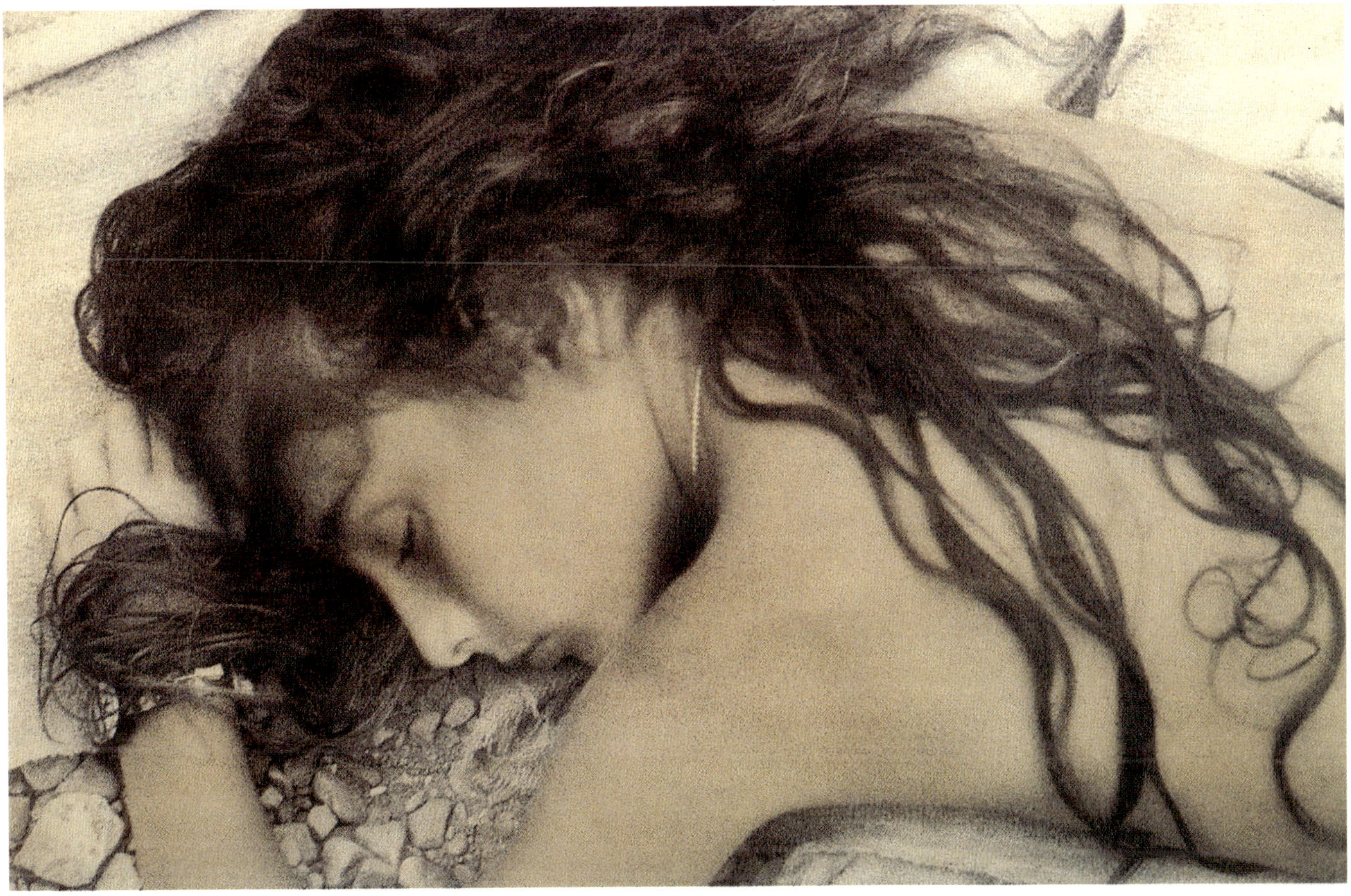

MAN RAY NUDE 1985

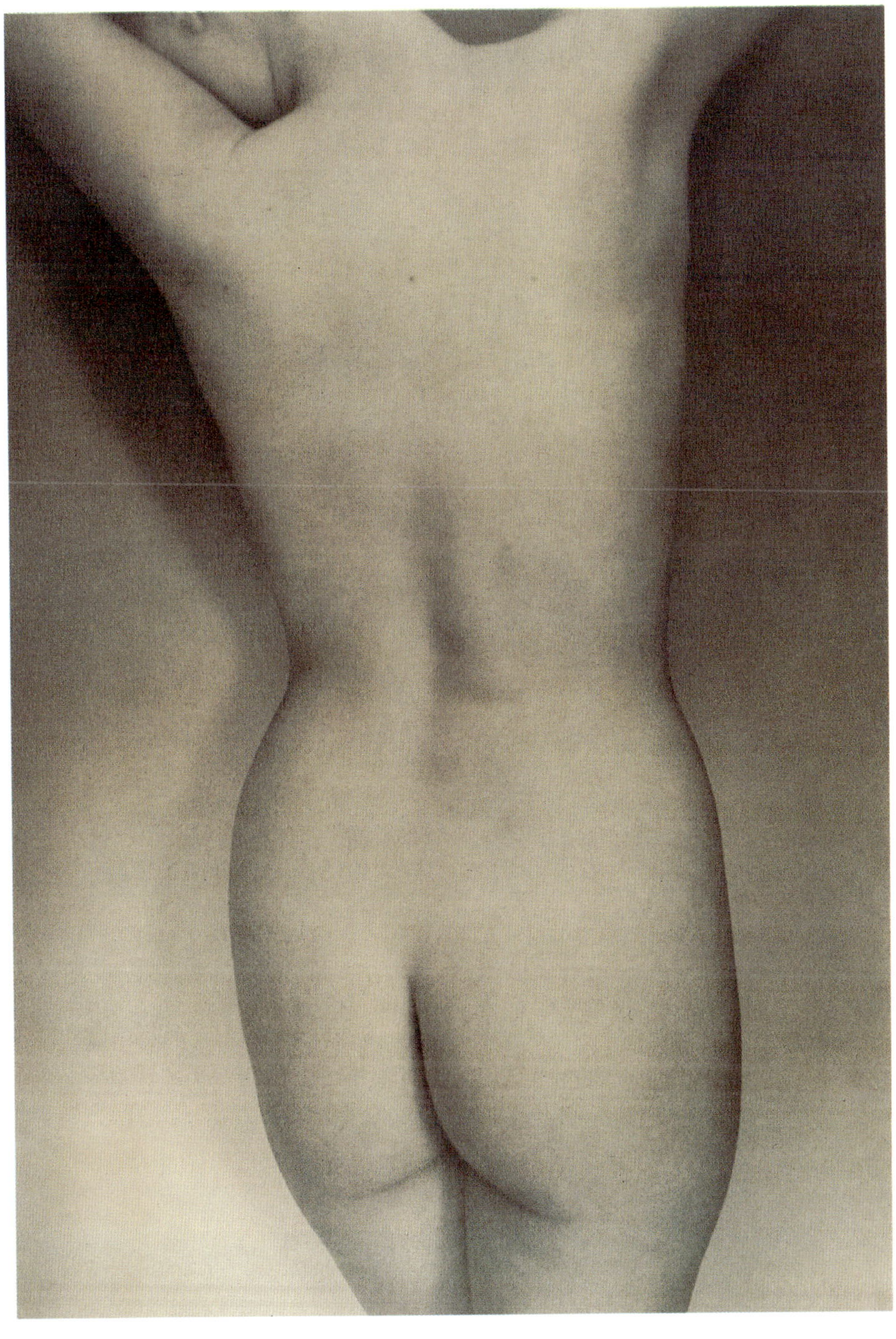

POINT OF IMPACT NUMBER I 1988

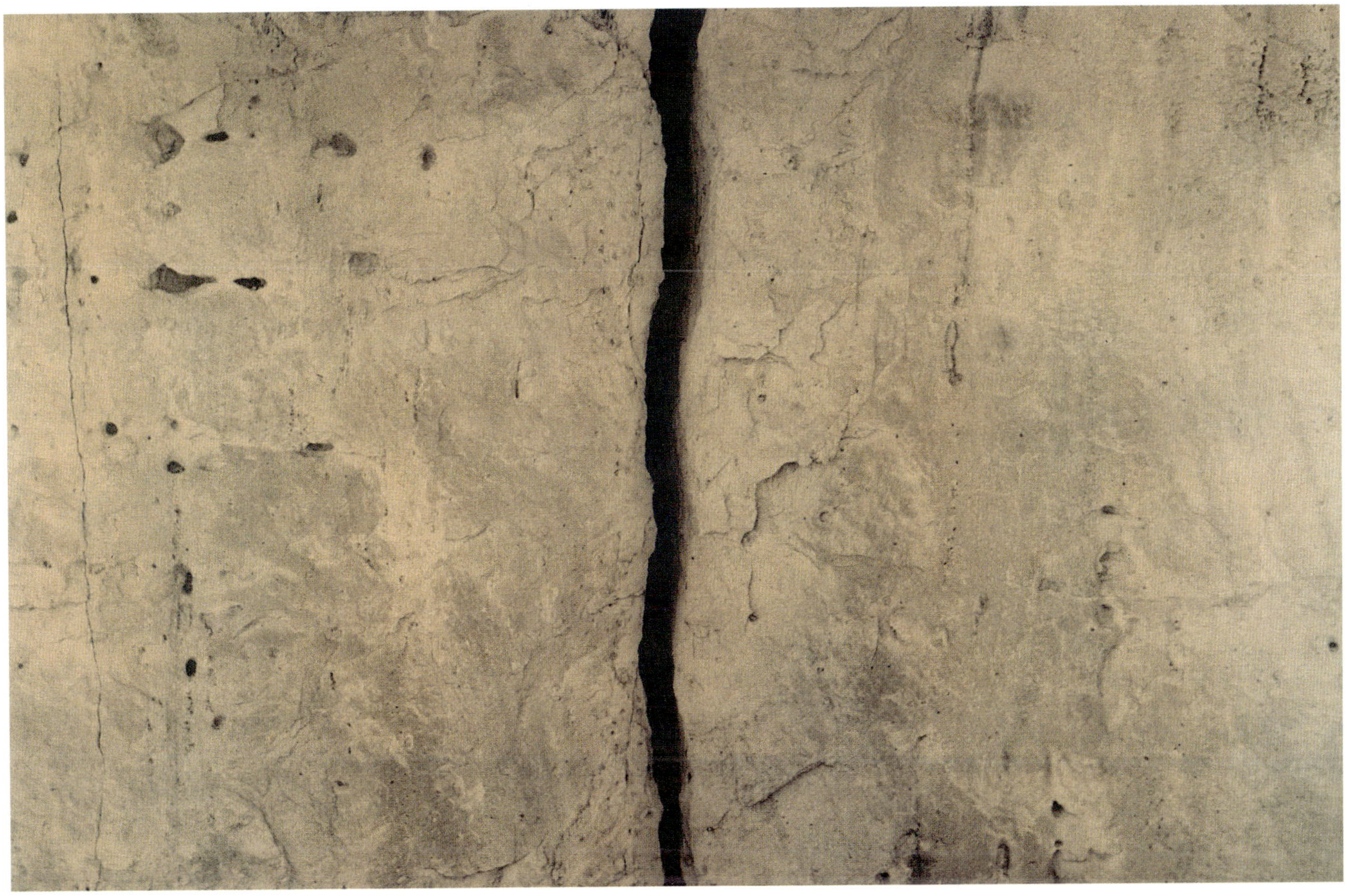

THE FALCON 1990

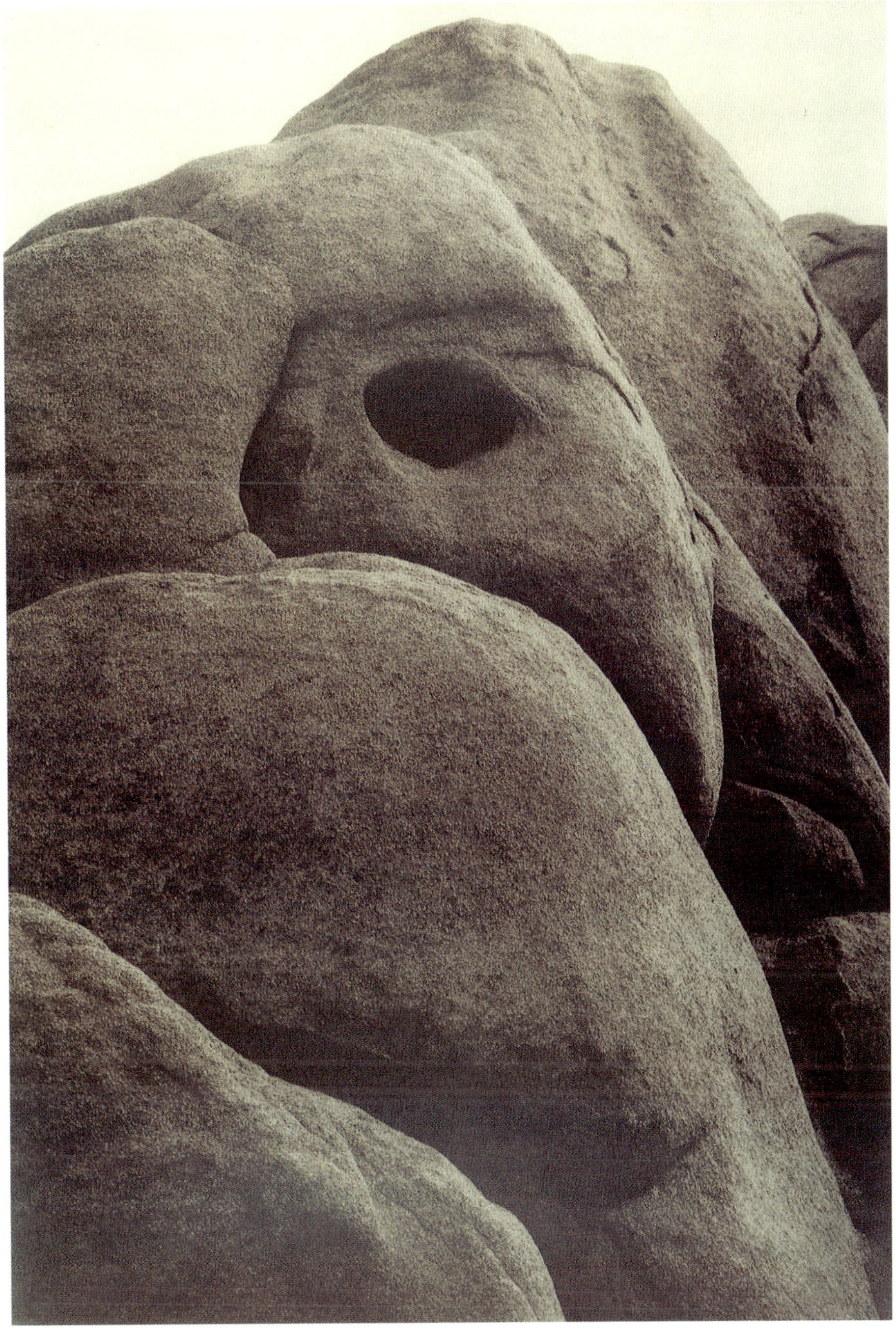

JOSIE, BODY PARTS 1991

JOSIE, BODY PARTS 1991

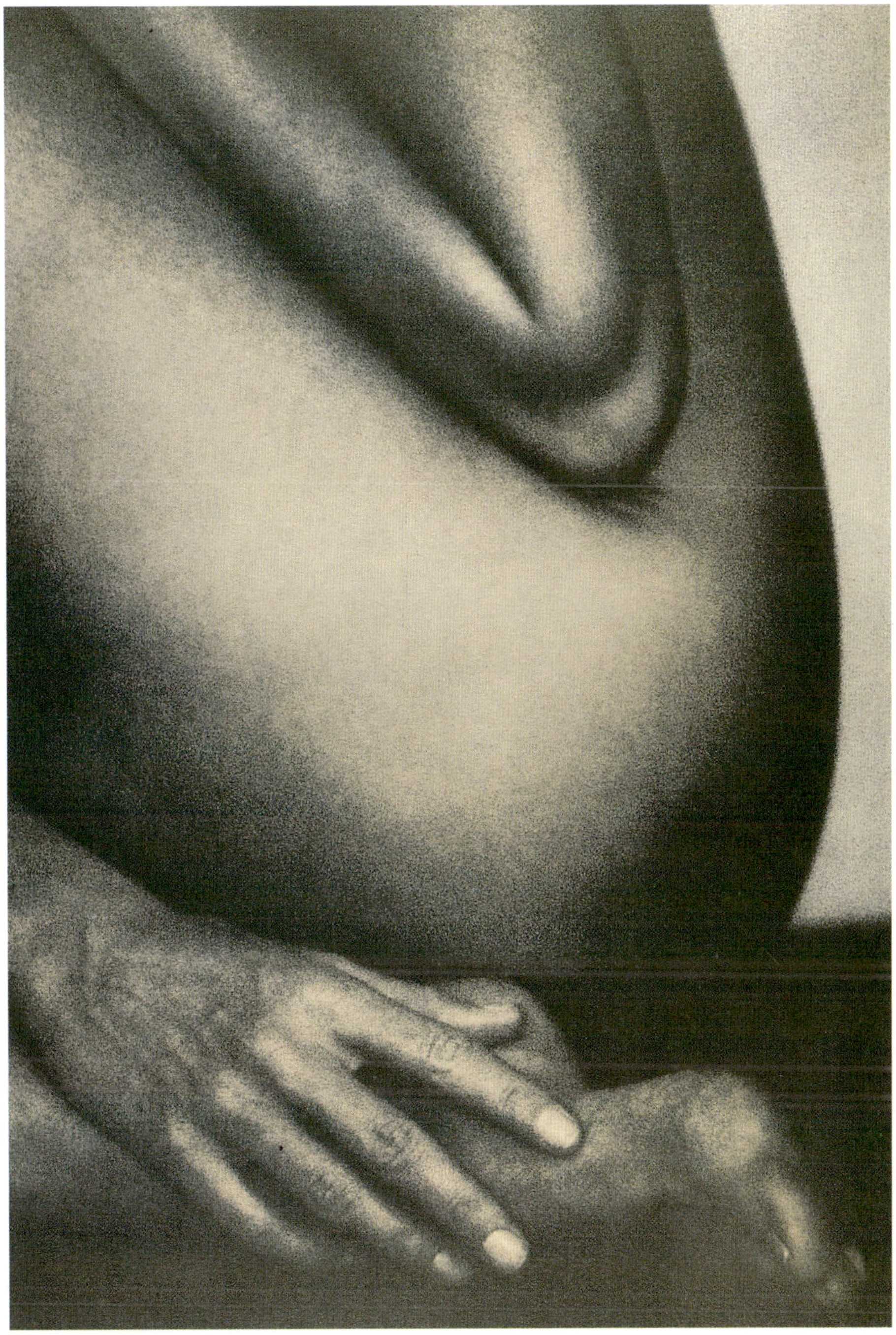

THE WHITE PLACE 1988

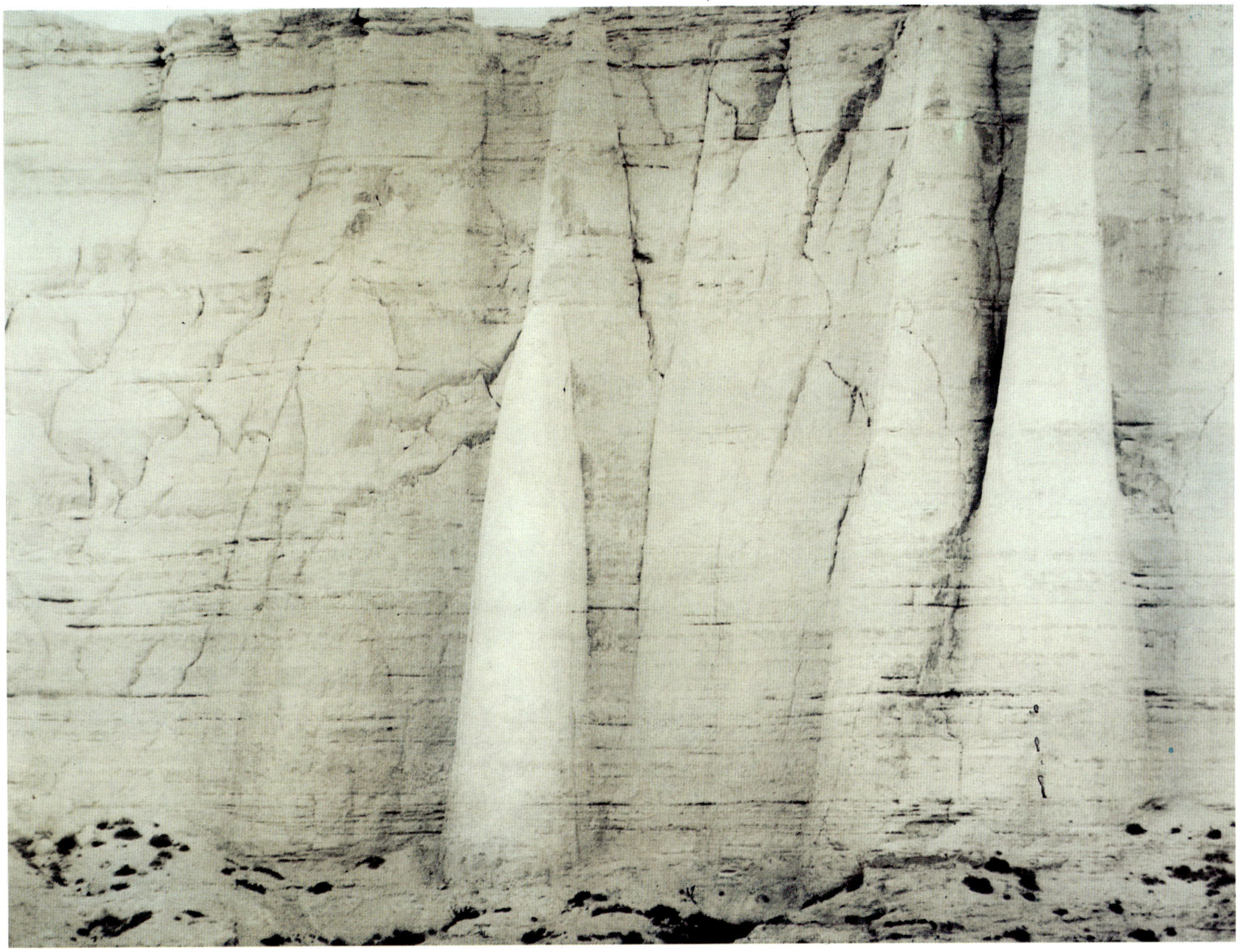

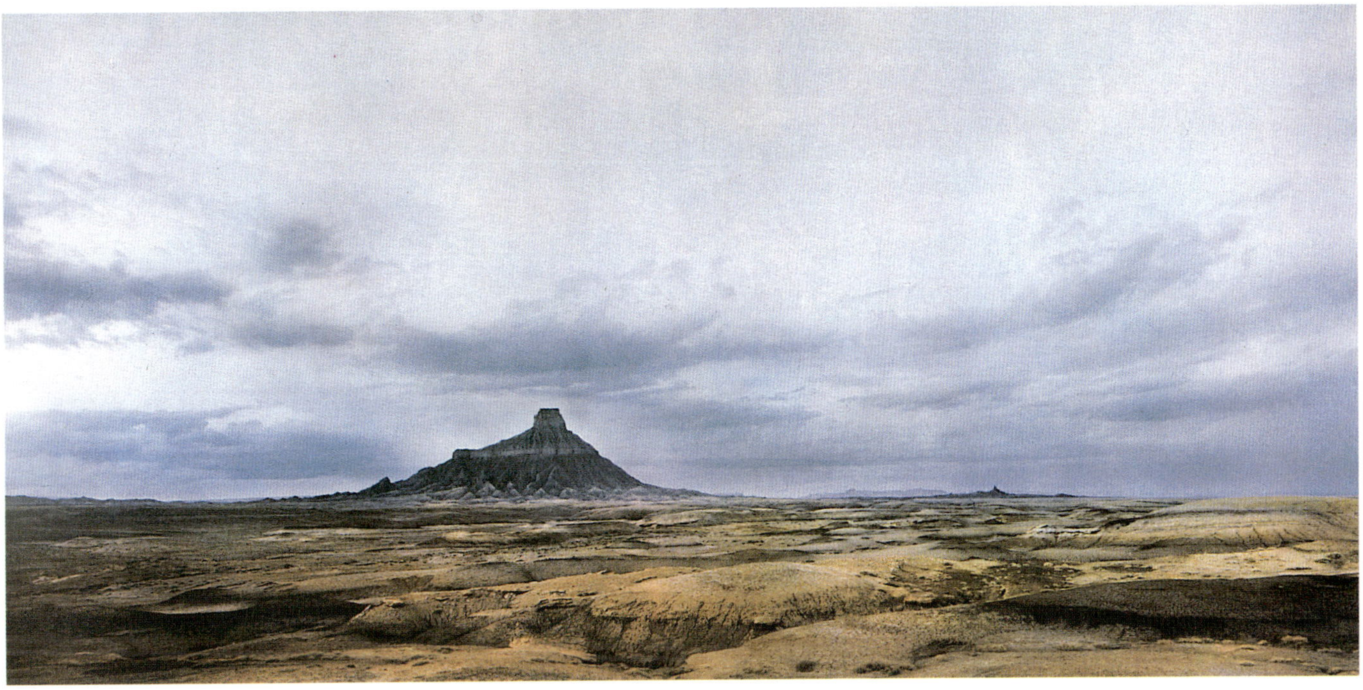

RED PLANET 1990

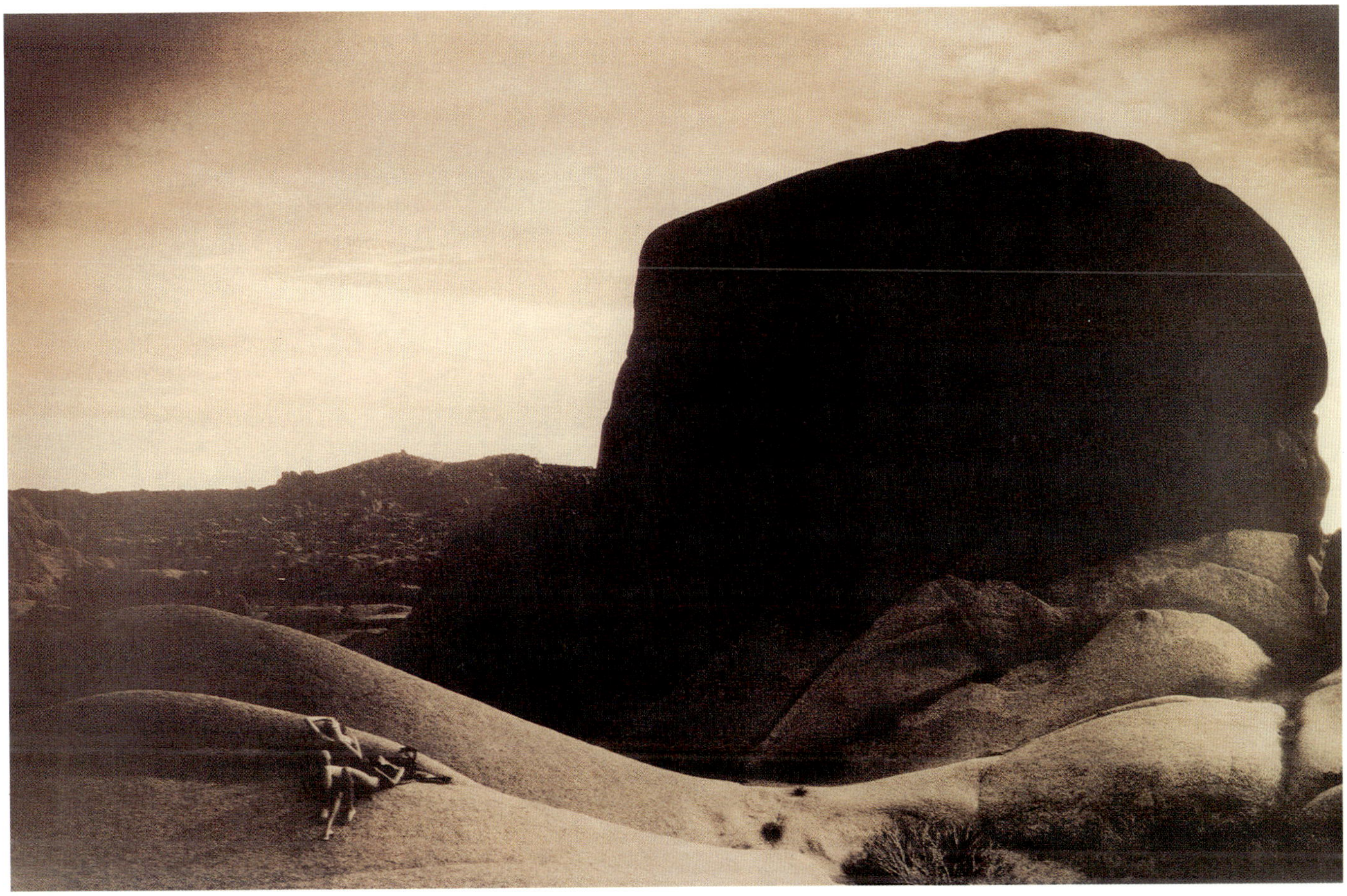

THE STORM 1990

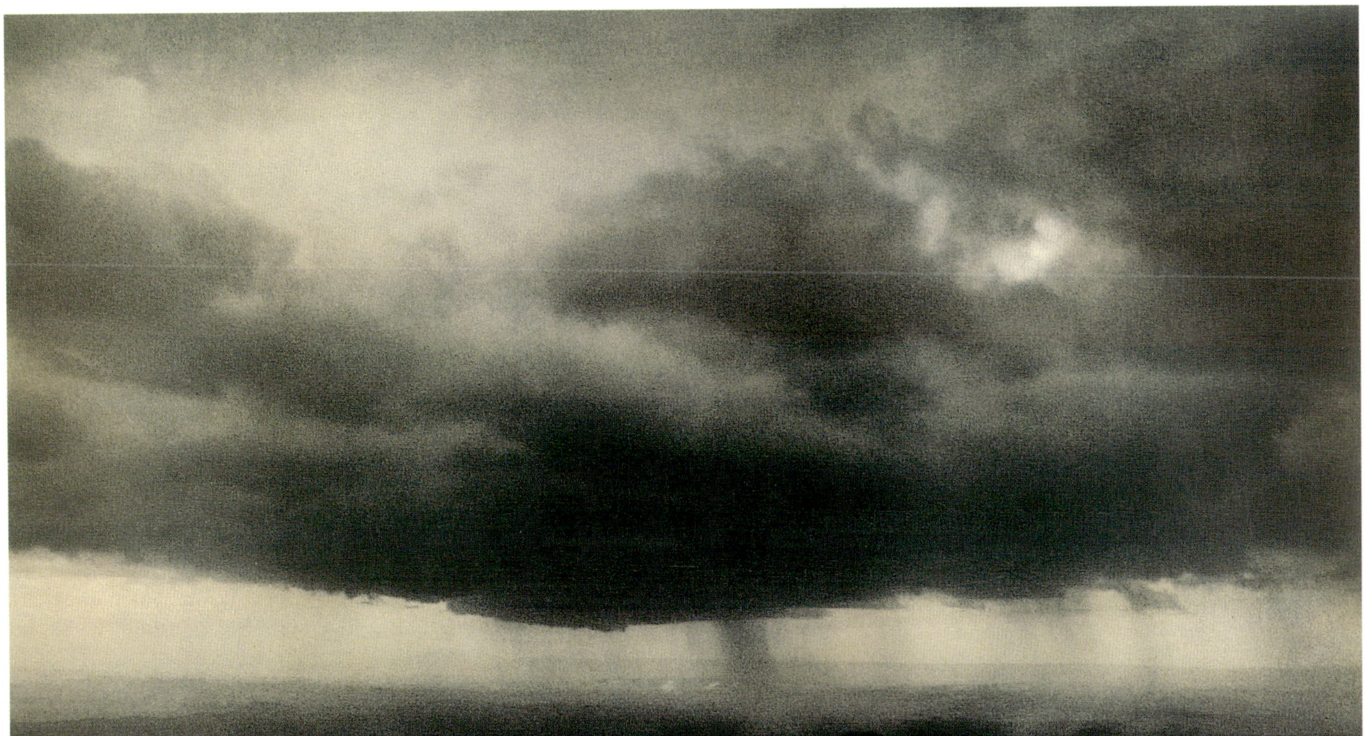

JOSIE, BODY PARTS 1991

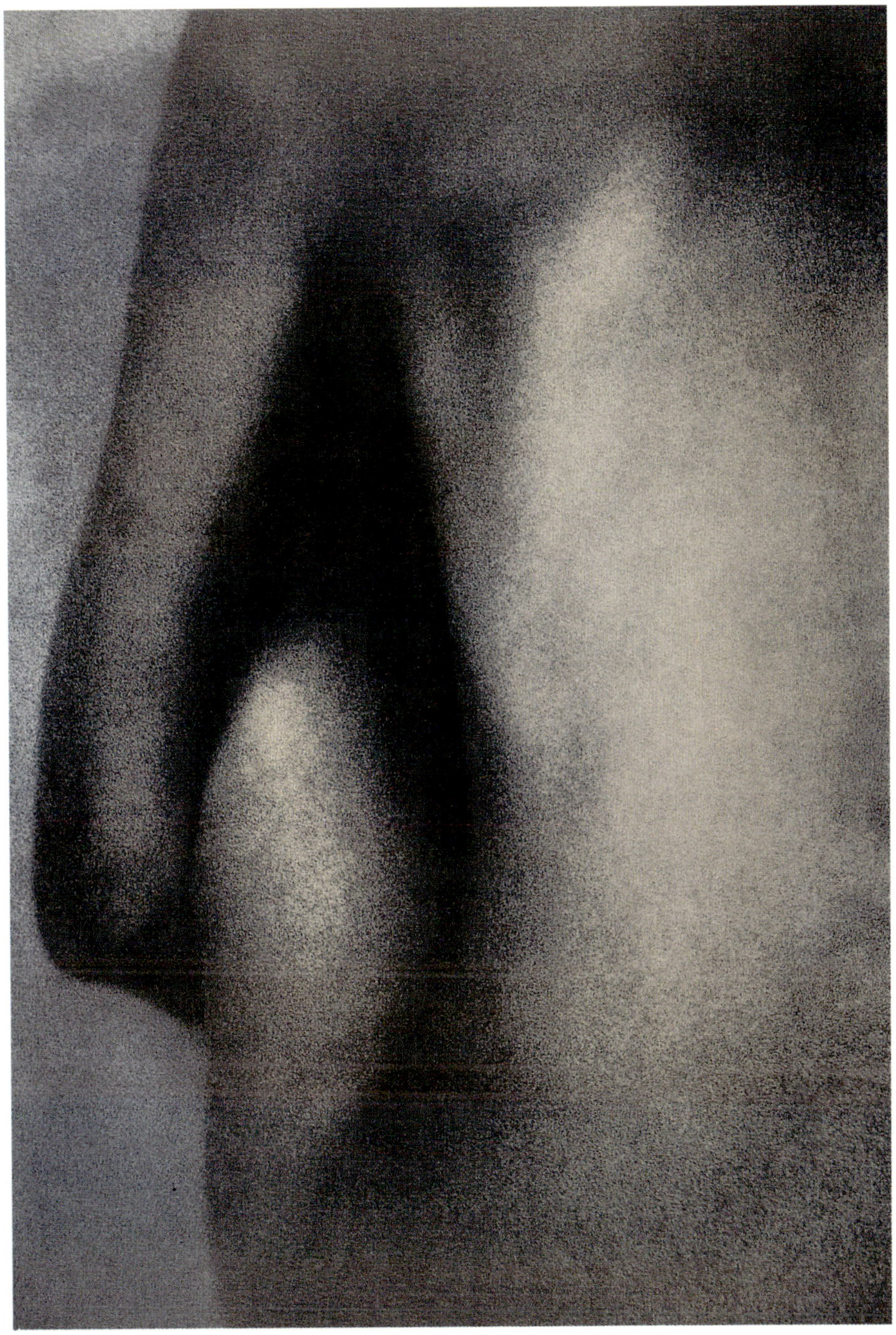

POINT OF IMPACT NUMBER 2 1988

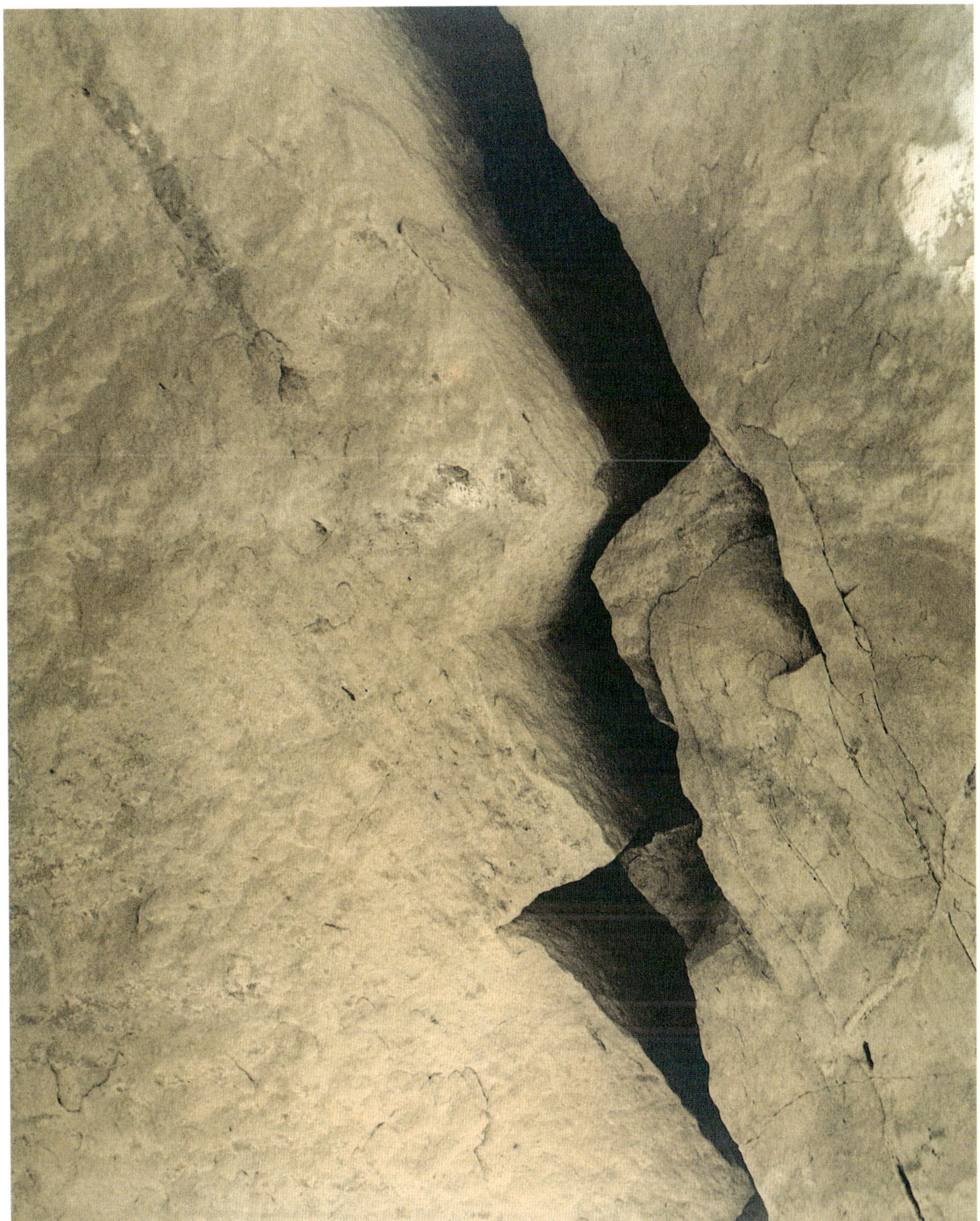

MAN RAY TULIP 1988

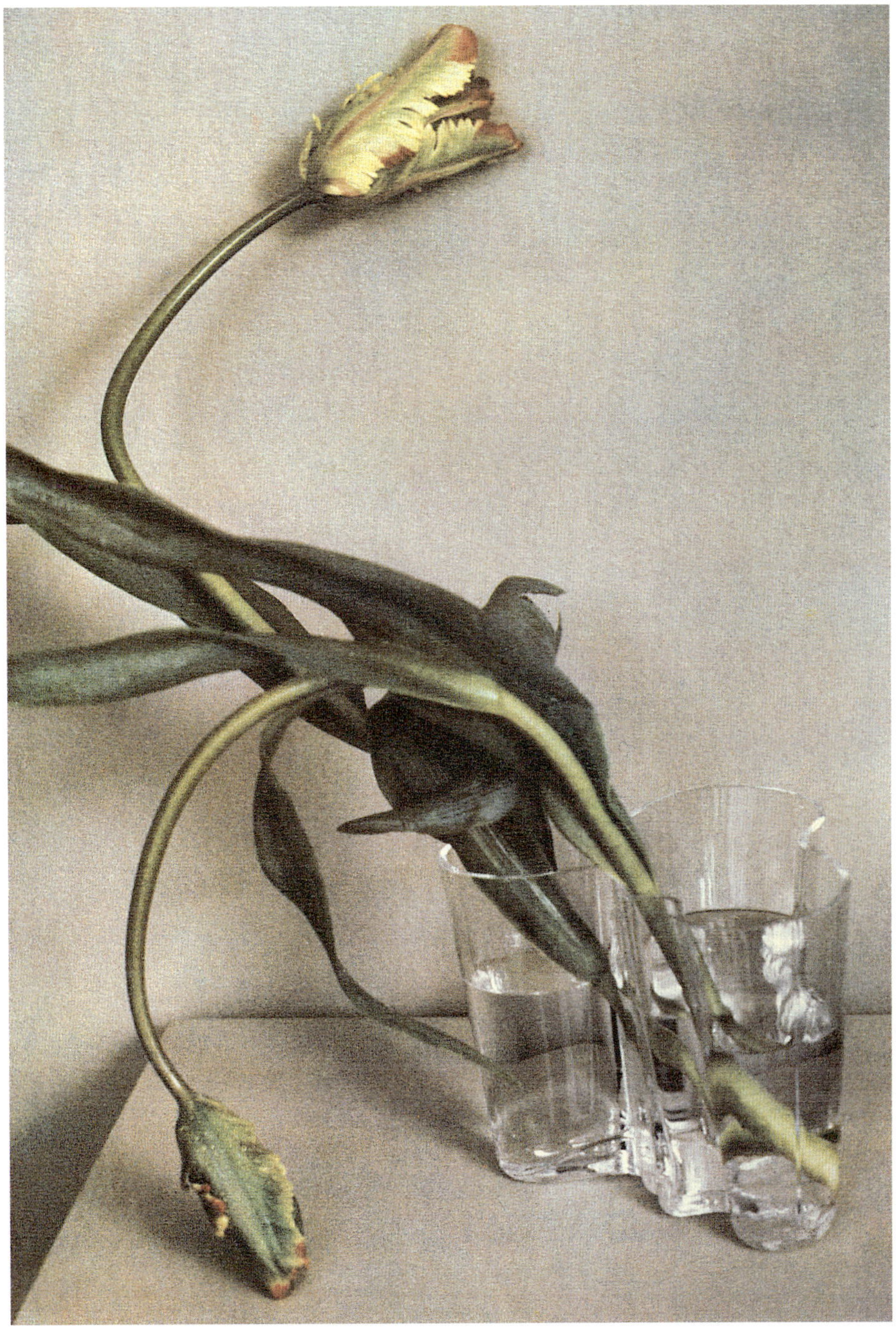

SUZUKI BOWL 1989

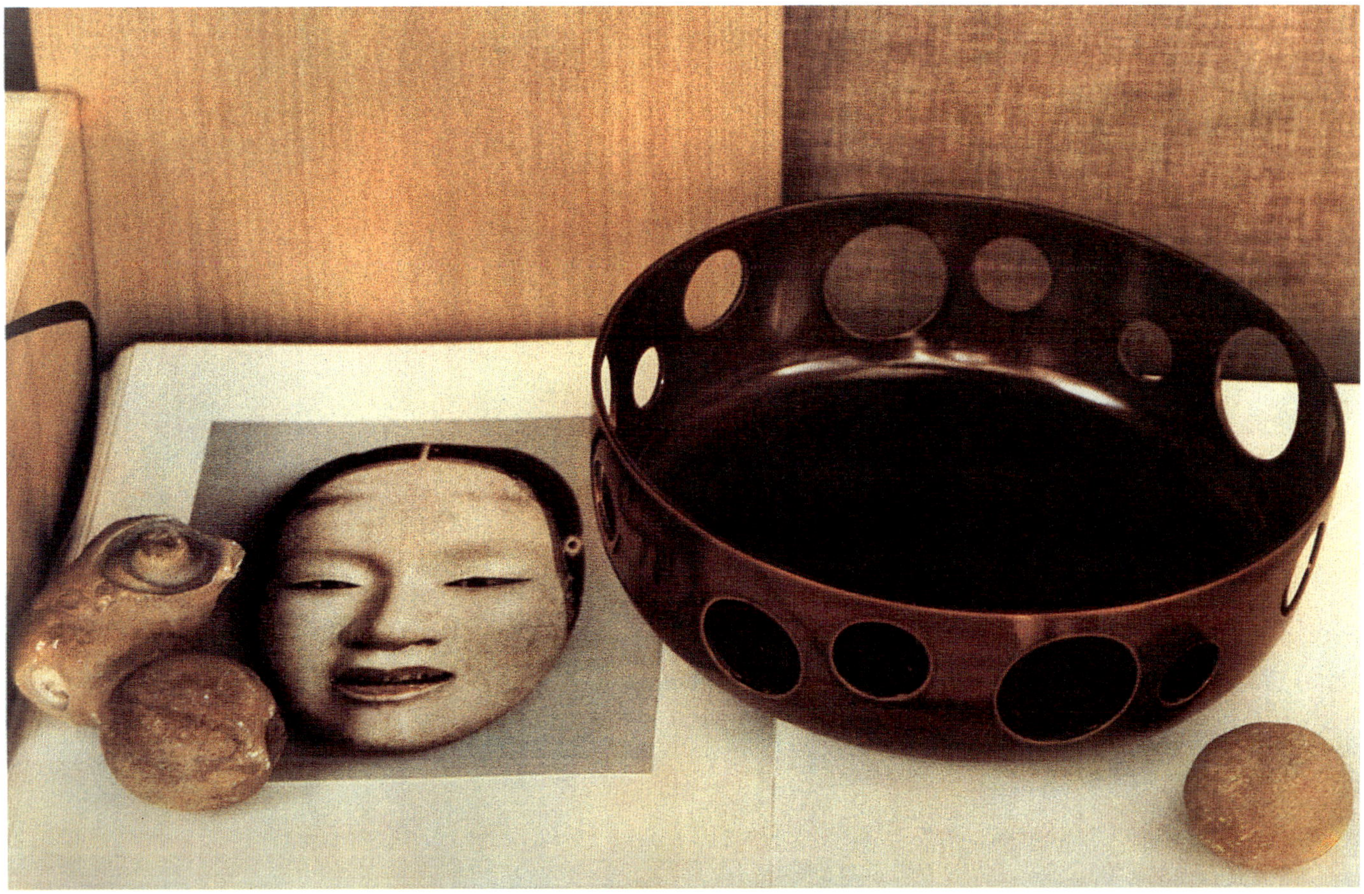

LYNN, NUDE 1990

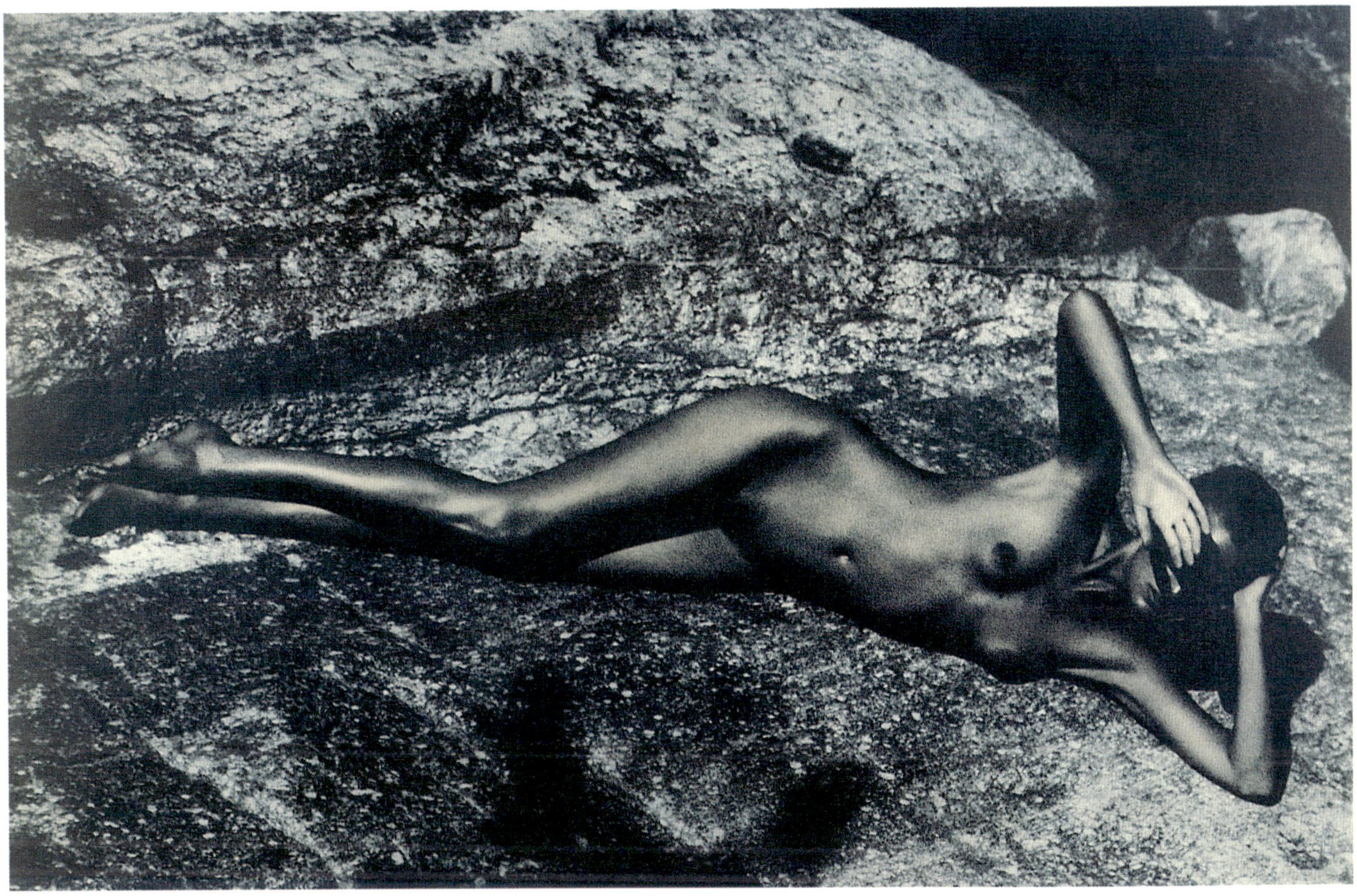

COLOSSUS RAMSES 1988

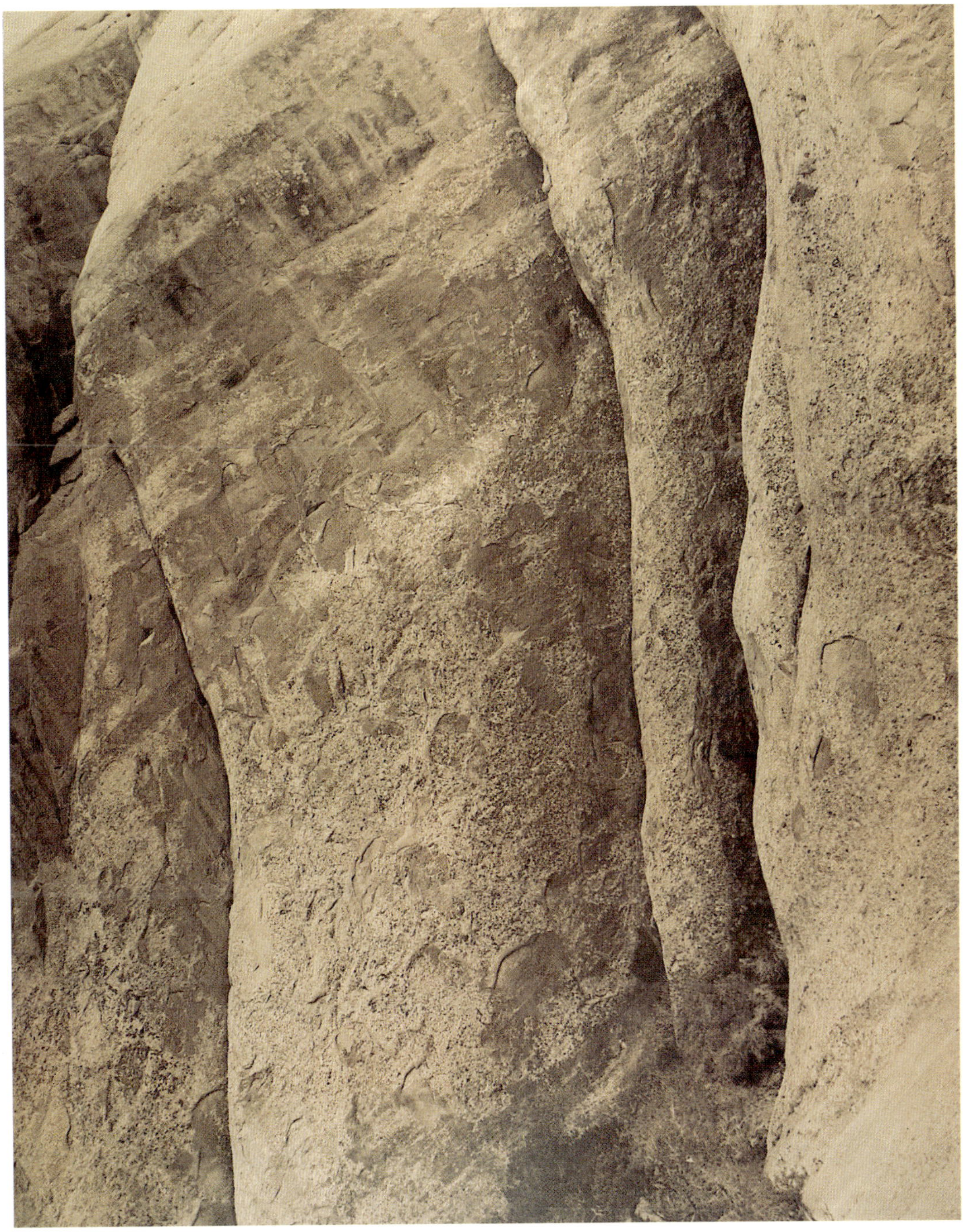

MARS 1988

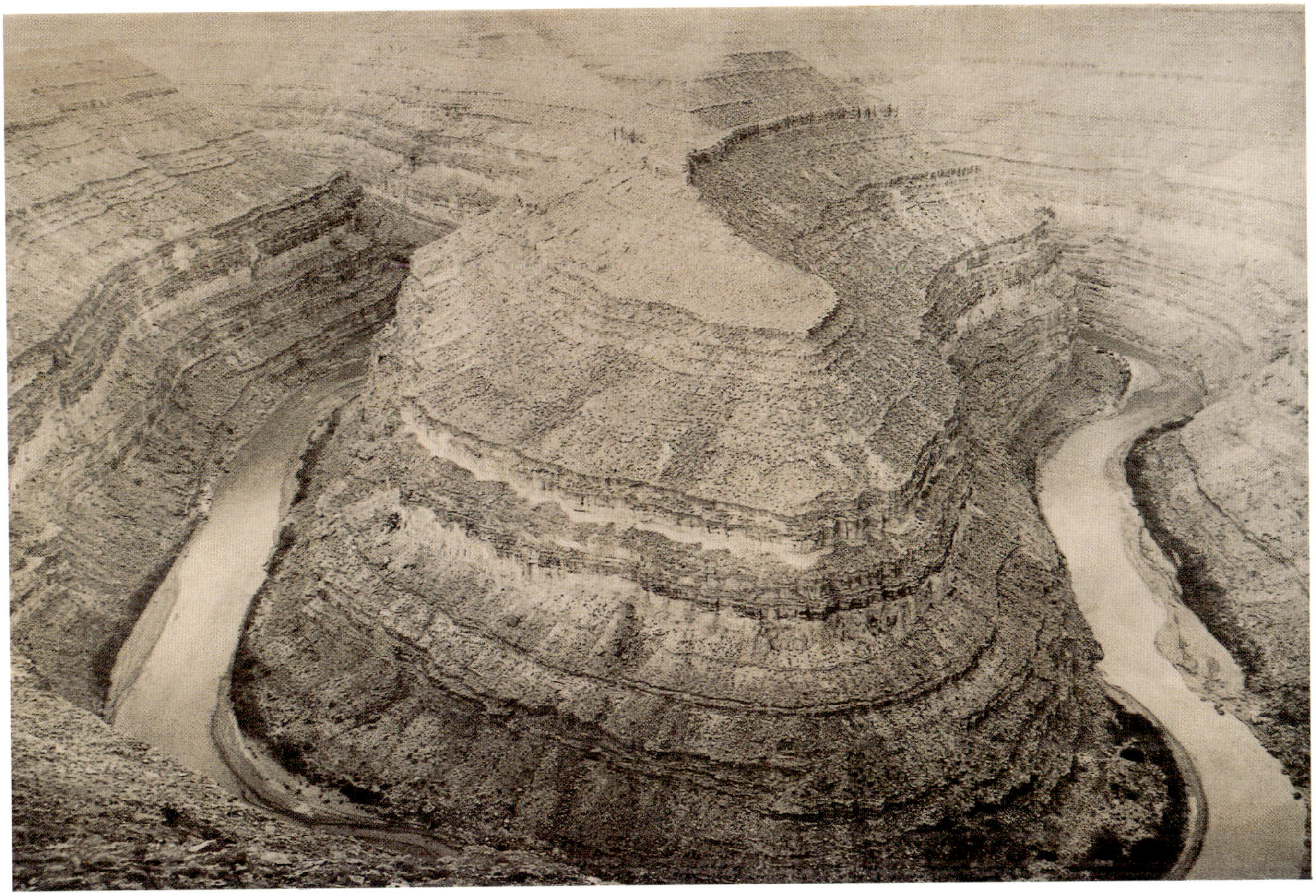

RAINBOW TURNED TO STONE 1990

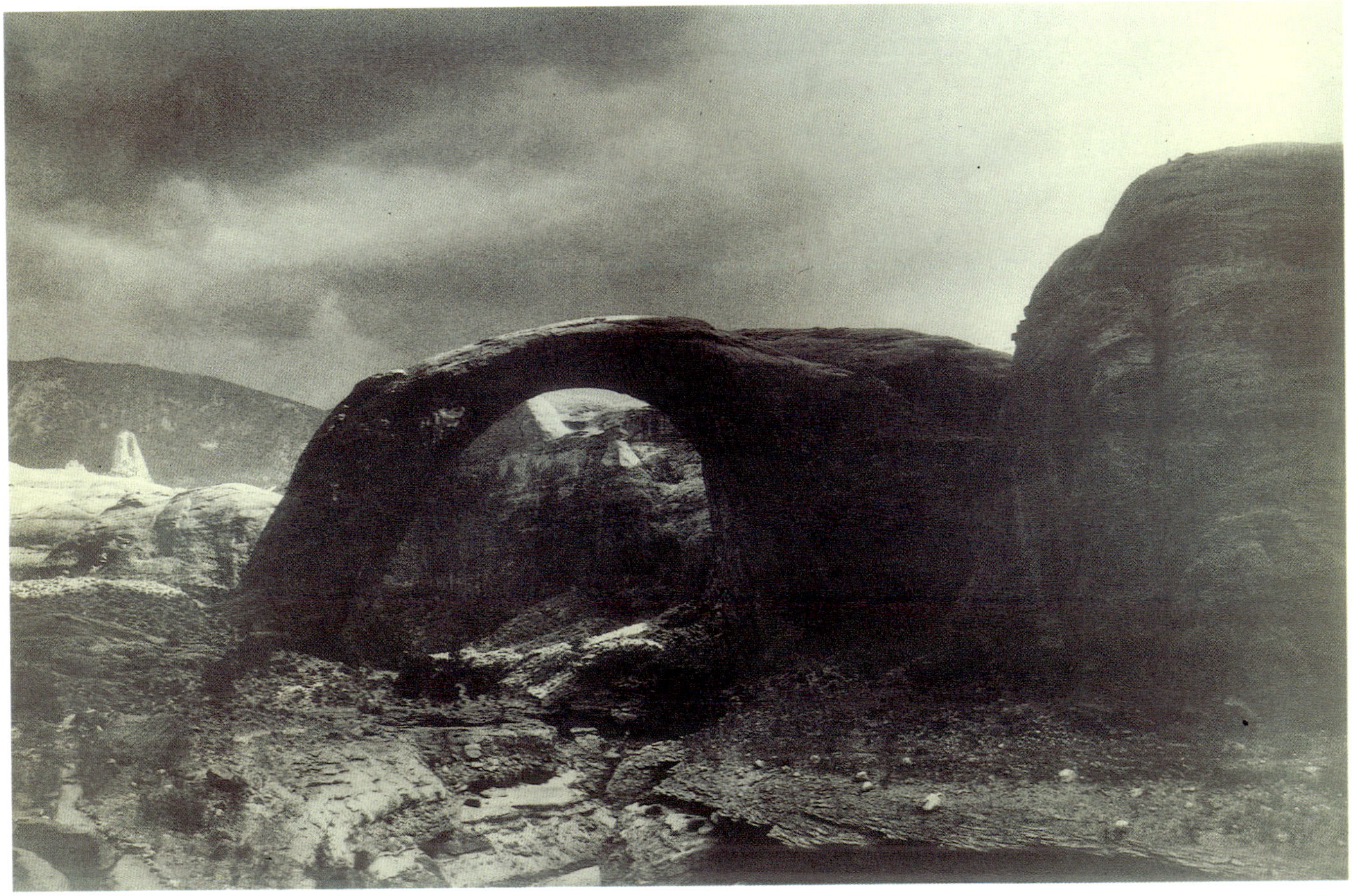

INDOMITABLE SPIRIT 1989

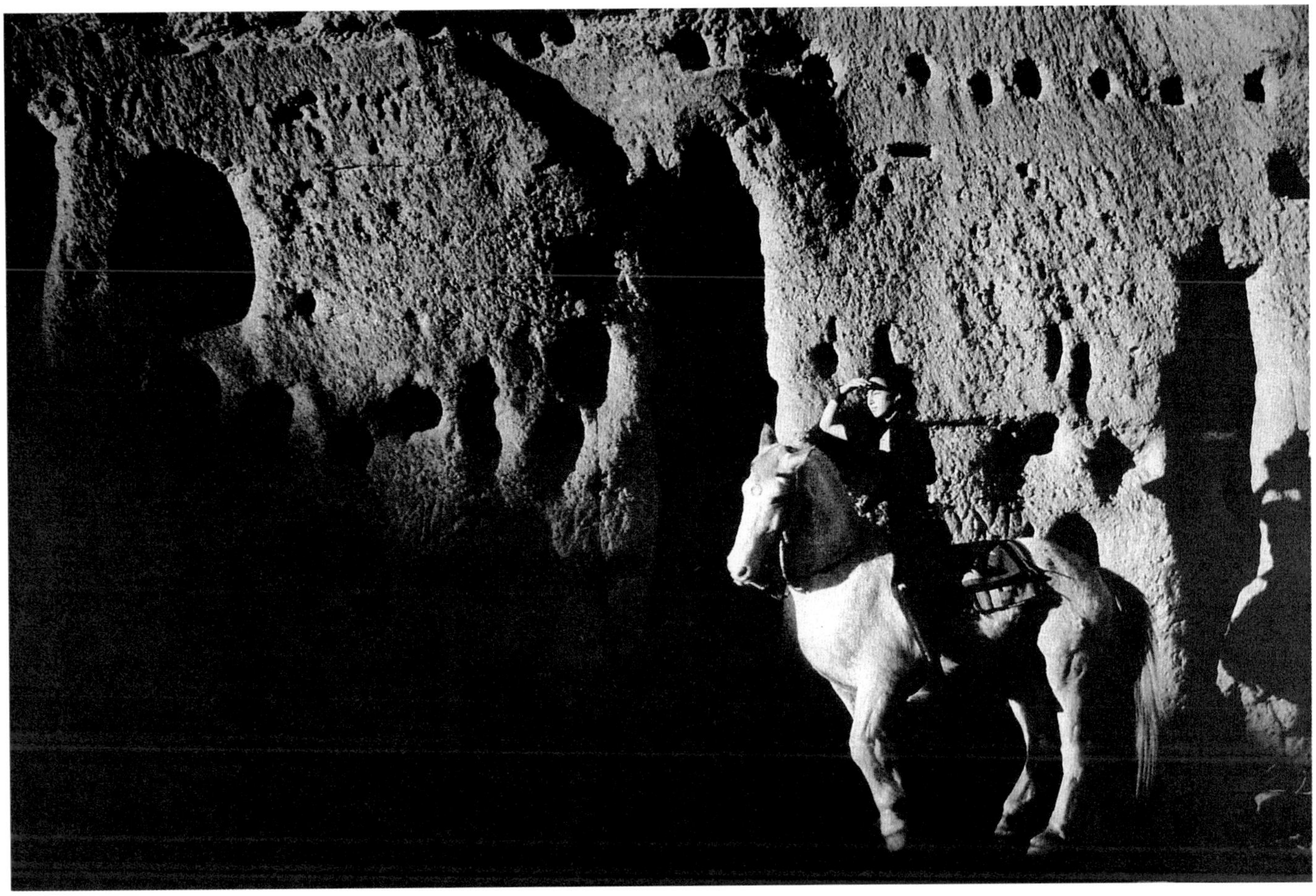

D'OU VENONS NOUS? QUE SOMMES-NOUS? OÙ ALLONS-NOUS?
PAUL GAUGUIN, 1897

IT IS NOT MY INTENTION TO GET INVOLVED WITH SENTIMENT BUT TO EXPRESS AN UNDERSTANDING OF MY PLACE IN RELATION TO THIS BOOK AND TO ACKNOWLEDGE ALL OF THE PEOPLE WHO CONTRIBUTED TO IT.

WE EXIST ON MANY LEVELS. IN OUR DAILY LIFE WE STRIVE, SUCCUMB TO JEALOUSIES, FIGHT, CURSE, LOVE AND SO ON. BENEATH THIS IS A THREAD WE CLING TO. A WISH FOR PEACE, ORDER, FREEDOM FROM DEATH, AND THE FEAR AND CHAOS OUT OF WHICH OUR WORKS ARISE. THE PEOPLE WHO HAVE WORKED WITH ME ON THE PICTURES IN THIS BOOK ARE CRAFTSMEN IN THEIR OWN FIELDS. ORIGINALLY STRANGERS, FRIENDSHIP HAS BECOME A PART OF THIS PROCESS. THE REST ARE FAMILY.

THE WORK OF ANY ARTIST IS ON THE SURFACE SINGULAR, SELFISH AND ONE'S OWN OBSESSION. BENEATH THE SURFACE IS MYSTERY AND A WISH FOR SOMETHING FINER AND HIGHER, A COLLABORATION OF HEARTS. THANK YOU FOR YOUR CONTRIBUTIONS AND I HOPE IN SOME WAY THIS BOOK REPRESENTS MY APPRECIATION FOR ALL YOU HAVE DONE.

SHEILA METZNER, APRIL 1991

TO MY HUSBAND JEFFREY
MY CHILDREN RAVEN, BEGA, RUBY, STELLA AND LOUIE
ALISON AND EVYAN
MY MOTHER AND MY FATHER

JACK WOODY
FOR INSISTING THAT THIS BE "HIS" BOOK

ATELIER MICHEL FRESSON—PROCÉDÉ PHOTO AU CHARBON
FOR THEIR CRAFT AND FOR THEIR
FINE PRINTS AND RELENTLESS EFFORTS ON MY BEHALF

NELL GUTMAN
FOR HER UTMOST DEDICATION

RICK DINOME
FOR HIS STRONG COMPANIONSHIP AND SUPPORT

ALEX FINDLAY
FOR KEEPING IT TOGETHER

AARON ROSE
FOR TEACHING ME THAT THE CAMERA IS A TOOL
AND PHOTOGRAPHY IS "PAINTING WITH LIGHT"

DAVID FAHEY
FAHEY/KLEIN GALLERY, LOS ANGELES

ALEXANDER LIBERMAN
ANNA WINTOUR

GERARD BOLLEI

ESTELLE JUSSIM
FOR THE "SOUTHWEST" SERIES

EELCO WOLF

CORNELL CAPA, WESTON NAEF, JOHN SZARKOWSKI
DANIEL WOLF, BONNI BENRUBI, DIANA EDKINS, JANE CORKIN
JAMES DANZIGER, KENNETH S. TARANTO, BEATRICE OST KUTTNER
LUDWIG KUTTNER, LISA AND ERIC EISNER, WARREN BEATTY
DELORENZO GALLERY, FIFTY/50, BARRY FRIEDMAN GALLERY
GALERIE METROPOL, STEVEN GREENBERG, CALVIN KLEIN
PURE MADDERLAKE, LES FLEURS DE MAXIM'S
PERLS GALLERIES, STALEY-WISE GALLERY

PRIMAVERA GALLERY
(AUDREY FRIEDMAN AND CHAIM MANISCHEVITZ)
BISHOP'S LODGE (JIM AND CAROL THORPE), SECOND HAND ROSE
FRED SILBERMAN, ARTWEAVE GALLERY
JOHN COOPER III, JACK LINDHOLM, PHILIPE ANGERS
STACEY FARNWORTH, CINDY GRABAU, DANIEL KUTTNER
HOLLISTER LOWE, ANDREW MEYERS
MARY GREENWELL, KEVYN AUCOIN, ANNE MARIE BARTHELEMY
MICHELE DE LA RUE, JOANNE GAIR, SONIA KASHUK
MARIE-JOSEE LAFONTAINE, LINDA MASON, LAURA MERCIER
GLORIA NATALI, ANDREA PAOLETTI, MARIE MADELEINE SAVIN
MICHELLE VOYSKI, GABRIELE VIGORELLI
MADELEINE COFANO, GIORGIO, DIDIER MALIGE, GERALD PORCHER
BOB RECINE, GABRIEL SABA, JOHN SAHAG
SAM MCKNIGHT, MARK GARRISON, PETER SAVIC, LARISA FALANGA
IRENE SILVAGNI, MARY SHANAHAN, LLOYD ZIFF
GRACE CODDINGTON, POLLY MELLEN, LINDA RODIN
GRACE MIRABELLA, PAUL SINCLAIRE, RIP GEORGES, RUTH ANSEL
CHARLES CHURCHWARD, ELIZABETH BIONDI, DEREK UNGLESS
FRANCA SOZZANI, ROBERT TURNER, ANGELICA BLECHSCHMIDT
PAULETTE DUFAULT, FENDI, KARL LAGERFELD
DAIMARU, JOHN JAY, KAORU WATANABE, KOTARO SUZUKI
HUEI AND YEN (M COMPANY), ALPHA CUBIC, QUEST
HIRO YAMAMOTO, JOSIE BORAIN, ELAINE IRWIN, UMA THURMAN
MARIE SOPHIE WILSON, LYNN SCHAUWECKER
ANA LUCIA ALVEZ PEREIRA, SCOTT BENOIT, KATHLEEN CARR
LAETITIA FIRMIN-DIDOT, NATALIE GABRIELLI, JOKO, LISA KALFUS
JOHN GRUBB MCCLASH, ROSEMARY MCGROTHA
MICHAL MARGULIES WEIDNER, HESTER WENZEL

SELECTED INDIVIDUAL EXHIBITIONS

DANIEL WOLF, INC., NEW YORK, NEW YORK 1978

STILLS: THE SCOTTISH PHOTOGRAPHY GROUP
EDINBURGH, SCOTLAND 1979

DANIEL WOLF, INC., NEW YORK, NEW YORK 1980

NIKON FOTO GALERIE, ZURICH, SWITZERLAND 1981

CLARENCE KENNEDY GALLERY, POLAROID CORPORATION
CAMBRIDGE, MASSACHUSETTS 1983

DANIEL WOLF, INC., NEW YORK, NEW YORK 1984

DANIEL WOLF, INC., NEW YORK, NEW YORK 1986

ROBERT KLEIN GALLERY, BOSTON, MASSACHUSETTS 1987

ROBERT KOCH GALLERY, SAN FRANCISCO, CALIFORNIA 1987

IDEE GALLERY, TOKYO, JAPAN 1987

P.P.S. GALLERY, HAMBURG, GERMANY 1988

JANE CORKIN, TORONTO, CANADA 1989

ROCHESTER INSTITUTE OF TECHNOLOGY
ROCHESTER, NEW YORK 1990

JAMES DANZIGER GALLERY, NEW YORK, NEW YORK 1990

HOUK GALLERY, CHICAGO, ILLINOIS 1991

FAHEY/KLEIN GALLERY, LOS ANGELES, CALIFORNIA 1991

INTERNATIONAL CENTER OF PHOTOGRAPHY
NEW YORK, NEW YORK 1991

DAIMARU GALLERY, TOKYO, JAPAN 1992

SELECTED GROUP EXHIBITIONS

MIRRORS AND WINDOWS: AMERICAN PHOTOGRAPHY SINCE 1960
MUSEUM OF MODERN ART, NEW YORK, NEW YORK 1978

PICTORIALISM
DANIEL WOLF, INC., NEW YORK, NEW YORK 1980

CONTEMPORARY COLOR PHOTOGRAPHY
THE CHRYSLER MUSEUM, NORFOLK, VIRGINIA 1981

COUNTERPARTS: FORM AND EMOTION IN PHOTOGRAPHS
METROPOLITAN MUSEUM OF ART, NEW YORK, NEW YORK 1982

COLOR AS FORM
GEORGE EASTMAN HOUSE, ROCHESTER, NEW YORK 1982

20TH CENTURY PHOTOGRAPHS FROM THE MUSEUM OF MODERN ART
SEIBU MUSEUM OF ART, TOKYO, JAPAN 1983

NEW YORK BY EIGHT PHOTOGRAPHERS
DANIEL WOLF, INC., NEW YORK, NEW YORK 1983

CONTEMPORARY PHOTOGRAPHY
ALBRIGHT KNOX ART GALLERY, BUFFALO, NEW YORK 1983

FLOWERS: AN EXHIBITION OF PHOTOGRAPHS
MONIQUE KNOWLTON GALLERY, NEW YORK, NEW YORK 1985

SWIMMERS
PACE / MACGILL, NEW YORK, NEW YORK 1985

FRESSON PHOTOGRAPHS: A UNITY OF VISIONS
NEW YORK, NEW YORK 1985

MASTERPIECES
JANE CORKIN, TORONTO, CANADA 1986

MIDTOWN REVIEW
INTERNATIONAL CENTER OF PHOTOGRAPHY, MIDTOWN
NEW YORK, NEW YORK 1986

PUBLIC / PRIVATE
MUSEUM OF CONTEMPORARY PHOTOGRAPHY
COLUMBIA COLLEGE, CHICAGO, ILLINOIS 1986

PUBLIC EXPOSURES, PRIVATE VISIONS
THE PHOTOGRAPHIC RESOURCE CENTER
BOSTON, MASSACHUSETTS 1986

CANON GALLERY, PARIS, FRANCE 1987

BOTANICA, PHOTOGRAPHIES DE VÉGÉTAUX
AUX XIXE ET XXE SIÈCLES
CENTRE NATIONAL DE LA PHOTOGRAPHIE
PARIS, FRANCE 1987

LEGACY OF LIGHT
INTERNATIONAL CENTER OF PHOTOGRAPHY, NEW YORK, NEW YORK 1987
NATIONAL PORTRAIT GALLERY, WASHINGTON, D.C. 1988

THE MODERNIST STILL LIFE — PHOTOGRAPHED
UNIVERSITY OF MISSOURI, ST. LOUIS, MISSOURI 1989

IMAGES OF ILLUSION
THE FORUM, ST. LOUIS, MISSOURI 1989

MODEFOTOGRAFIE VON 1900 BIS HEUTE
KUNSTFORUM LANDERBANK, VIENNA, AUSTRIA 1990

THE INDOMITABLE SPIRIT
PHOTOGRAPHERS AND FRIENDS UNITED AGAINST AIDS
INTERNATIONAL CENTER OF PHOTOGRAPHY, MIDTOWN
NEW YORK, NEW YORK 1990
THE LOS ANGELES MUNICIPAL ART GALLERY
LOS ANGELES, CALIFORNIA 1990

PHOTOGRAPHERS' MUSES
JAMES DANZIGER, NEW YORK, NEW YORK 1990

SELECTED PUBLIC COLLECTIONS

THE METROPOLITAN MUSEUM OF ART
NEW YORK, NEW YORK

THE MUSEUM OF MODERN ART
NEW YORK, NEW YORK

INTERNATIONAL CENTER OF PHOTOGRAPHY
NEW YORK, NEW YORK

THE CHRYSLER MUSEUM, NORFOLK, VIRGINIA

POLAROID CORPORATION, BOSTON, MASSACHUSETTS

AGFA CORPORATION, RIDGEFIELD PARK, NEW JERSEY

MUSEUM OF FINE ARTS, HOUSTON, TEXAS

BOOKS

MIRRORS AND WINDOWS: AMERICAN PHOTOGRAPHY SINCE 1960
JOHN SZARKOWSKI, THE MUSEUM OF MODERN ART
NEW YORK, NEW YORK 1978

NUDE: PHOTOGRAPHS 1850-1980
CONSTANCE SULLIVAN, HARPER AND ROW
NEW YORK, NEW YORK 1980

COUNTERPARTS: FORM AND EMOTION IN PHOTOGRAPHS
WESTON J. NAEF, THE METROPOLITAN MUSEUM OF ART
NEW YORK, NEW YORK 1982

PORTRAITS: THE GALLERY OF WORLD PHOTOGRAPHY
COLIN FORD, EDITOR, SHUEISHA PUBLISHING CO., LTD.
TOKYO, JAPAN 1983

NEW TRENDS: THE GALLERY OF WORLD PHOTOGRAPHY
WESTON J. NAEF, EDITOR, SHUEISHA PUBLISHING CO., LTD.
TOKYO, JAPAN 1984

HUMAN FIGURE: THE GALLERY OF WORLD PHOTOGRAPHY
DAVID HERBERT, EDITOR, SHUEISHA PUBLISHING CO., LTD.
TOKYO, JAPAN 1984

NEW DIRECTIONS: THE GALLERY OF WORLD PHOTOGRAPHY
WESTON J. NAEF, EDITOR, SHUEISHA PUBLISHING CO., LTD.
TOKYO, JAPAN 1984

THE INTERNATIONAL CENTER OF PHOTOGRAPHY ENCYCLOPEDIA
I.C.P., A POUND PRESS/CROWN PUBLISHERS, INC. BOOK
NEW YORK, NEW YORK 1984

OBJECTS OF DESIRE, SHEILA METZNER
CONSTANCE SULLIVAN, EDITOR, A POLAROID BOOK
CLARKSON N. POTTER, NEW YORK, NEW YORK 1986

BOTANICA, PHOTOGRAPHIES DE VÉGÉTAUX
AUX XIXE ET XXE SIÈCLES
PREFACE: PIERRE GASCAR
CENTRE NATIONAL DE LA PHOTOGRAPHIE
PARIS, FRANCE 1987

LEGACY OF LIGHT
CONSTANCE SULLIVAN, EDITOR, A POLAROID BOOK
ALFRED A. KNOPF, NEW YORK, NEW YORK 1987

THE MODERNIST STILL LIFE-PHOTOGRAPHED
JEAN S. TUCKER, UNIVERSITY OF MISSOURI
ST. LOUIS, MISSOURI 1989

NEW YORK FASHION, THE EVOLUTION OF AMERICAN STYLE
CAROLINE RENNOLDS MILBANK, HARRY N. ABRAMS, INC.
NEW YORK, NEW YORK 1989

THE INDOMITABLE SPIRIT
PHOTOGRAPHERS AND FRIENDS UNITED AGAINST AIDS
PREFACE: ANDY GRUNDBERG; INTRODUCTION: MARVIN HEIFERMAN
HARRY N. ABRAMS, INC., NEW YORK, NEW YORK 1990

ARTICLES

DELIBERATELY OLD-FASHIONED
GENE THORNTON, THE NEW YORK TIMES, NOVEMBER 26, 1978

THE PERSISTENCE OF PICTORIALISM
CARTER RATCLIFF, ART IN AMERICA, SEPTEMBER 1980

NATURE MORTE
ALEXANDRA ANDERSON, CAMERA ARTS, JANUARY-FEBRUARY 1981

SHEILA METZNER: STYLED ON THE PAST
CAROL SQUIERS, MODERN PHOTOGRAPHY, OCTOBER 1981

SHEILA METZNER
HASSE PERSSON, FOTO (SWEDISH), FEBRUARY 1982

THE PERCEPTUAL FANTASIES OF SHEILA METZNER
MAX KOZLOFF, CLOSE-UP, POLAROID CORPORATION, AUGUST 1982

LOOKING FOR THE PRESENT
ESTELLE JUSSIM, THE BOSTON REVIEW,
FEBRUARY 1984, VOLUME IX, NUMBER I

TIME STANDS STILL
ESTELLE JUSSIM, AFTERIMAGE, MARCH 1984

NEW LIGHT ON COLOR
SUSAN WEILEY, ART NEWS, OCTOBER 1985

SHEILA METZNER
PHOTO JAPON, ISSUE #10, FALL 1986

ART LIFE
THE NEW YORKER, DECEMBER 8, 1986

PHOTOGRAPHY THROUGH THE FANTASY VISION
OF SHEILA METZNER'S PRISM
ABIGAIL FOERSTNER, CHICAGO TRIBUNE, JANUARY 9, 1987

WHAT BECOMES AN ARTIST MOST
GINGER DANTO, ART NEWS, NOVEMBER 1987

SHEILA METZNER'S PHOTOGRAPHY: IN SEARCH OF THE SACRED
STYLING, DECEMBER 1987, NUMBER 10

METZNER'S MAGIC
PHOTO DISTRICT NEWS, JANUARY 1988, VOLUME VII, ISSUE I

SHEILA METZNER
HG, JUNE 1988

SHEILA METZNER
NUDE 2, SUMMER 1988

150 YEARS OF PHOTOGRAPHY, PORTFOLIO
ART NEWS, APRIL 1989

REINVENTING PHOTOGRAPHY
CELEBRATING 150 YEARS OF THE MEDIUM
ART & ANTIQUES, MAY 1989

SHEILA METZNER
NUDE 3, SUMMER 1989

ZOOM ANNIVERSAIRE, SUMMER 1989

THE ADVERTISING GAME
AMERICAN PHOTO, JULY/AUGUST 1990

PHOTOGRAPHY
THE NEW YORKER, AUGUST 6, 1990

OBJECTS OF DESIRE: SHEILA METZNER
CAROL SQUIERS, AMERICAN PHOTO
NOVEMBER/DECEMBER 1990

PUTTING ON THE STYLE
INTERVIEWS BY PATRICIA NORRIS
THE LONDON SUNDAY TIMES MAGAZINE, APRIL 7, 1991

BODY LANGUAGE
PENELOPE GREEN, THE NEW YORK TIMES MAGAZINE, MAY 5, 1991

CREDITS

UMA, PATOU DRESS 1986
REPRODUCED COURTESY BRITISH VOGUE
© CONDÉ NAST PUBLICATIONS, LTD.

FENDI HUOMO 1988
COURTESY PARFUMS FENDI

THE PASSION OF ROME 1986
COURTESY PARFUMS FENDI

MARIE SOPHIE 1986
COURTESY PARFUMS FENDI

MARIE SOPHIE 1986
COURTESY PARFUMS FENDI

MARIE SOPHIE 1986
COURTESY PARFUMS FENDI

ELAINE, LEE MILLER 1988
COURTESY VOGUE PARIS

KATHLEEN CARR 1985
COURTESY BLOOMINGDALES

ART DECO LADY 1984
COURTESY VOGUE, COPYRIGHT © 1984
BY THE CONDÉ NAST PUBLICATIONS, INC.

ROSEMARY, BRACELETS 1984
COURTESY VOGUE

RED PLANET 1990
SHEILA METZNER FOR GERMAN VOGUE

MOUILLE, PROTOTYPES 1985
COURTESY DELORENZO GALLERY

COLOPHON

THE FIRST EDITION OF
SHEILA METZNER; COLOR
IS LIMITED TO TEN THOUSAND CASEBOUND BOOKS

A SPECIAL EDITION OF ONE HUNDRED BOOKS
IS SLIPCASED, NUMBERED AND SIGNED BY THE ARTIST

DESIGN IS BY JACK WOODY
THE TYPEFACE IS GARAMOND
THE PLATES ARE FOUR COLOR OFFSET
PRINTED ON A MATTE COATED PAPER STOCK
PRINTED AND BOUND IN SINGAPORE
FOR

TWIN PALMS PUBLISHERS
2400 NORTH LAKE AVENUE
ALTADENA, CALIFORNIA 91001
818-798-3116

ISBN 0-944092-15-2

1991